A GUIDE TO EVERYDAY ECONOMIC STATISTICS

GARY E. CLAYTON
Northern Kentucky University

MARTIN GERHARD GIESBRECHT
Northern Kentucky University

McGRAW-HILL PUBLISHING COMPANY

New York St. Louis San Francisco Auckland Bogotá Caracas Hamburg Lisbon London Madrid Mexico Milan Montreal New Delhi Oklahoma City Paris San Juan São Paulo Singapore Sydney Tokyo Toronto

A GUIDE TO EVERYDAY ECONOMIC STATISTICS

1 2 3 4 5 6 7 8 9 0 DOCDOC 8 9 3 2 1 0 9

ISBN 0-07-011299-1

The editor was Scott D. Stratford;
the production supervisor was Denise L. Puryear.
R.R. Donnelley & Sons Company was printer and binder.

Library of Congress Cataloging-in-Publication Data

Clayton, Gary E.
A Guide to everyday economic statistics.
1. Economics–Statistical methods. I. Giesbrecht, Martin Gerhard, (date). II.Title.
HB137.C57 1990 330'.021 89-14515
ISBN 0-07-011299-1

To our loving wives,

Jonna and Pat,

and our wonderful children and family members,

Clayt, Kimberly, Brandon, Darren and Mindy

Lisa, Marty, Ted and Tom

Table of Contents

Preface

There is something exciting about economic statistics. Although they may be expected to be, like so many other statistics, about as dry as an old bus schedule, a closer look reveals them to be quite fascinating.

There are two reasons for this. One, economic statistics hit us where it counts: in the breadbasket, in our wallets, in our standards of living, and in our careers. And two, the statistics themselves are the product of one of the more extraordinary human endeavors of our modern age.

This book takes a closer look at them. It examines how the statistics are constructed and how they may be used. Like a road map, this book examines where they lead.

Statistics tell us a great deal about ourselves and our economy. Indeed, studying economics without paying attention to the statistics would be like a tourist trying to understand the lay of the land without consulting a road map. But this book is neither a statistics lecture nor an economics textbook.

Nor does it need to be read consecutively from beginning to end, although it lends itself well to that approach. It is a handy guide that can be consulted for clarification whenever any of the statistical series dealt with herein are encountered.

Use it well, and use it often.

Gary E. Clayton
Martin Gerhard Giesbrecht

Chapter 1
INTRODUCTION

Why We Need Economic Statistics

How is business?

How is the economy?

If we were to ask these same questions about our own personal health, the answer would be based largely on our own personal experiences. Most of the time, we don't need a medical doctor to tell us that we are feeling well when we feel well, nor do we need a doctor to tell us that we have a headache when we have a headache. But sometimes we need more information about our health than we can generate by ourselves. Blood tests and x-rays can tell us some things about ourselves that we never could have guessed or suspected otherwise.

The same is true with the economy. We often rely on our own experience to determine how the economy is doing. If we are doing well -- good job, promising future, and maybe even some solid investments -- and if our experience is borne out by the successes of our friends and acquaintances, then we have compelling evidence that business is good and that the economy is doing well. Conversely, if the picture is less bright, then business and the economy may be in for some trouble.

But sometimes we need more information about the overall health of the economy than we can generate by ourselves. We need other indicators about business and economic conditions, and these other indicators can also give us information that we could never have guessed otherwise.

That is why we need economic statistics.

How the Statistics in This Book Were Chosen

There are literally millions of statistical series that could serve as indicators of economic well-being. At the personal level, each of us could probably generate a dozen series from our grocery receipts, odometer readings, telephone bills, and electricity bills. Every business, town, city, county, and industry could and often does the same in its own field of operation.

Even the broad-based measures of economic statistics, those that deal with whole states, regions, and nations, number into the thousands. A glance at any statistical yearbook or almanac or at the annual Statistical Abstract of the United States[1] will make this point.

Yet, only 35 series of economic statistics are dealt with in this book. Why?

First and most obvious, there is such a thing as too much information. It can prevent us from seeing the forest for all the trees.

[1] Available from the Superintendent of Documents, U.S. Government Printing Office, Washington, D.C. 20402, Telephone: (202)783-3238, or any U.S. Department of Commerce district office.

Second, many statistical series, like one detailing our own personal electric consumption, are not interesting to everyone. This is not to say they are not important! Hog price statistics make a big difference to midwestern farmers, and the annual data on deliveries of aircraft catch the attention of people living in Seattle where the big Boeing plant is located. But, you are encouraged to pursue special interests on your own.

Third, many statistical series are compiled and published too late to be of much more than historical interest. For example, median family income statistics are noteworthy because they are not distorted by a few very high incomes at the upper end of the range, and because family incomes are often a more realistic determinant of the standard of living than individual incomes.[2] However, as useful as the median family income statistical series is for social analysis and for understanding past economic trends, the most recent figures are generally published too late to be a major indicator of what is happening in the economy at this moment.

Finally, many statistical series are not reported regularly in the press and broadcast media. The implicit price deflator is a case in point. While important, the deflator, and many other series as well, is not readily available to people who don't happen to be working in major libraries, economic research centers, government agencies, banks, and other financial institutions.

The 35 series dealt with in this book are those with extremely high profiles. Some, like the Dow Jones Industrial Average, are reported daily -- on television, radio, and in national and local

---

[2] As a measure of central tendency, the median is less affected than the mean by distortions at either end of the scale.

newspapers. Others, like the prime rate, are mentioned less frequently but receive prominent attention when they do change.

Even just these 35 are usually more than enough. They include most of the major economic indicators that are important all of the time. The gross national product, the consumer price index, and the unemployment rate would certainly be in the top half dozen of anyone's list of key economic statistics. Many others are important most of the time, and the rest are, at least, important some of the time.

We may not have selected everyone's favorite statistical series -- and for this we apologize -- but we are driven by a positive philosophy of wanting to describe "what is," rather than a normative one of "what should be." Many statistics are neglected when they should not be, while others are widely reported when there is less reason to do so. However, the objective here is to provide a guide to those series that *do* receive attention, rather than the ones that *should* receive the acclaim.

A Frame of Reference

The main measure of overall economic and business activity is the gross national product (GNP), whose fluctuations are the most important gauge of good times or bad times that we have. In this context, as in virtually all others, GNP is to be understood as a final, bottom line accounting measure, an economic result, rather than as an indicator of things to come.

Many of the statistics reviewed in this book measure either the whole or parts of GNP. Other statistics, the index of leading indicators preeminent among them, serve better as signals of things to come. There are also the more specialized series, such as new private housing permits or the New York Stock Exchange composite, that serve both as general indicators of future economic activity and as first order indicators for their own industries. Finally, we have other series such as domestic auto sales that provide important information for their respective industries but have almost no value as an indicator of future economic activity.

As we peruse the formal world of economic statistics, bear in mind that they cannot be evaluated in a vacuum. Statistical series need a background, or a frame of reference, so they can be put in proper perspective. This the book attempts to do. Sometimes the frame of reference is discussed in terms of the historical development and evolution of the series. Or, the perspective takes the form of a detailed discussion of the way the statistic is measured and compiled. The frame of reference may also be in the way the particular indicator or statistic relates to other developments in the economy. In the end, our goal is to provide a perspective that allows for proper interpretation and application of the particular series.

To help develop your perspective, we have provided a number of charts, illustrations and tables so you can formulate your own opinions. One technique used extensively in this book is to superimpose the respective series on a background that shows recessions as shaded areas and periods of economic growth or expansion as unshaded areas. As can be seen in Figure 1-1, this allows us to compare changes in both the timing and magnitude of the series with changes in the overall economy. While this method is admittedly casual, it does provide a reasonably good picture of some fundamental relationships between the overall economy and the series in question.

Of particular interest in Figure 1-1 are the three types of indicators: leading, lagging, and coincident. The name given to each refers to the way the series moves in relation to changes in overall economic activity. For example, the series marked "leading indicator" turns down before the economy enters a recession and up before the expansion begins.

Figure 1-1
Leading, Coincident, and Lagging Indicators

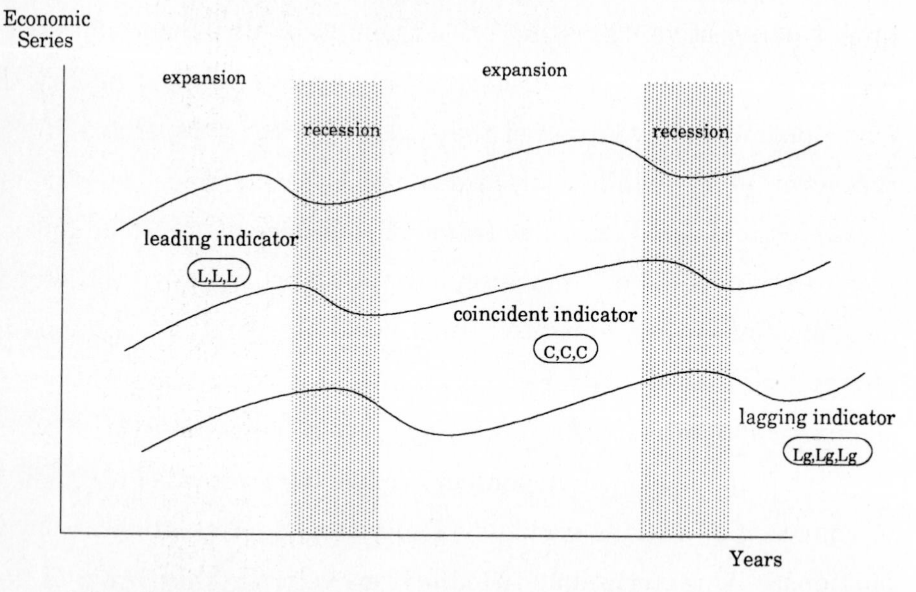

The "lagging indicator" series behaves just the opposite: it turns down after the economy enters a recession, and up sometime after the recovery is underway. A coincident indicator exhibits neither leads nor lags. Instead its timing is such that it turns down when the economy turns down and up when the economy turns up.

The three codes in the oval key for each indicator show how the changes in the individual series compare to changes in the overall economy. The coding is the same used by the Bureau of Economic Analysis (BEA) in the Department of Commerce to classify the economic indicators reported in the monthly Business Conditions Digest.

The first code stands for the timing of the series with respect to peaks in the economy, or when the expansion ends and the recession begins. The second stands for the timing of the series with respect to troughs in the economy, or when the recession ends and the recovery begins. The last code indicates the overall classification of the indicator. Some of the codes you will see in this book are as follows:

(L,Lg,U)

The series leads the peaks in the economy, or turns down before the economy turns down (L = leads).

The series lags the economic recovery, or turns up after the economy turns up (Lg = lags).

Overall, the series is unclassified; it is neither a leading nor a lagging indicator on a consistent basis (U = unclassified).

(C,Lg,U)

The series peaks when the economy peaks (C = coincident).

The series recovers after the economy recovers (Lg = lags).

Overall is unclassified (U = unclassified) as an economic indicator. It neither leads nor lags the economy on a regular basis.

(Lg,C,Lg)

The series lags the peaks in the economy, or turns down after the economy turns down (Lg = lags).

The series turns up at the same time the economy turns up (C = coincident).

Overall classification is a lagging indicator (even though the timing of the series is coincident for recoveries).

Sometimes a series leads both peaks and troughs in the economy to make it an overall leading indicator. At other times, it may lead peaks and lag troughs to earn an overall rating of "unclassified." Even other series play no role as an indicator of overall economic activity, so no codes are shown.

Whenever possible, the economic series examined in this book are plotted against the historical background of recessions and expansions. As will be seen, many series behave like those in Figure 1-1, although the timing of the turning points will vary considerably. Others will appear to have little, if any, relationship to changes in the overall economy. Even so, we feel that the presentation is important if you are to make your own judgments about the behavior of the series.

We have also listed convenient sources of data, sometimes in the form of easily accessible publications and sometimes in the form of a telephone hotline, to help you keep abreast of your own favorite series.

The Many Faces of Economic Statistics

The task of interpreting statistics might seem to be a simple one: just take the numbers and describe how they changed. Unfortunately, it's not always that easy. Sometimes a change in a series is significant because it affects so many other segments of the economy. Interest rates are a case in point since they affect (almost) everything from housing and automobiles to the cost of servicing the national debt. The task of interpretation is also made difficult because almost any statistical series can be reported in a number of ways.

To illustrate, consider a hypothetical report stating that manufacturers' inventories increased from $350 billion to $360 billion over a recent one-month period. If the report is in terms of current prices -- and many initial reports are released this way -- then it stands to reason that some of the $10 billion increase is due to inflation.

To compensate for inflation, inventories can also be measured in terms of constant dollars -- also known as real dollars -- using the prices that prevailed at a certain point in time. If 1982 is used as the base year, then the same report could be worded like this: "In terms of constant 1982 dollars, manufacturers' inventories increased from $270 billion to $277 billion for the most recent month." Since prices were about 30 percent lower in 1982 that they are today, the $350 billion is converted to $270 billion for purposes of the report.

It may seem odd to measure the value of today's inventories in terms of prices that are nearly ten years old, but the technique does remove the distortions of inflation. The new numbers, $270 and $277 billion respectively, are not very meaningful in terms of today's prices, but it is clear that the increase of $7 billion is real in the sense that it could not have been caused by inflation.

Most series that are susceptible to the distortions of inflation are reported in both current (nominal) and real dollar amounts, with 1982 being the most popular base year. Both kinds of information are valuable -- if used correctly -- although the availability of both means that final inventory statistics can be reported in a number of different ways:

* the current or *nominal* dollar value of total inventories ($360 billion)
* the *change* in the *nominal* dollar value of total inventories ($10 billion)
* the constant, or *real* dollar value, of total inventories ($270 billion)
* the *change* in the constant, or *real value*, of total inventories ($7 billion)
* the *percentage change* in *nominal* dollar inventories (2.86%, or $10 billion/$350 billion)
* the *percentage change* in *real* dollar inventories (2.59%, or $7 billion/$270 billion)

We run into the same type of problem when numbers are converted to an index, such as the consumer price index, the producer price index, or any number of other indices. For example, suppose that the index under consideration has a base year of 1977 = 100 and currently stands at 145. If the index goes to 146 in the next month, there is a 1 percent increase over the base period activity, or a .69 percent increase in the index over the previous month (1/145 = .0069). If the index were to grow at the same rate for each of the next 11 months, the annualized rate would be 8.6 percent.[3]

Using the numbers in the paragraph above, we can see that any index series, not just the index of industrial production, can be reported in several different ways:

---

[3] The series is *compounding* monthly, so the correct computation is to use the following formula:

$$\text{Annualized growth} = (1 + \text{monthly percentage change})^{12} - 1$$
$$= (1 + .0069)^{12} - 1 = .086$$

Because of compounding, you *cannot* multiply the monthly percentage change of .0069 by 12 to get an annualized rate, although some have made this mistake!

* the *absolute level* of the index (145)

* the *absolute change* in the level or the index from period to period (1)

* the *relative percentage change* from the previous period (.69%)

* an *annualized projection* of the current period percentage change (8.6%)

In general, the relative percentage change is the most useful, with the annualized version coming in next. However, the reader should be advised that even these lists are not exclusive. For example, sometimes the change in the level of the index is compared to a period 12 months earlier. If the new level of 146 is 10 points higher than it was 12 months ago, then we could also say that the annual increase was closer to 7.35%.

Abusing Economic Statistics

When we consider the enormous quantity and variety of economic statistics, as well as the number of formats in which each can be reported, it is not surprising that they are sometimes abused. Several examples are worthy of mention.

Perhaps the most common abuse of economic statistics is to apply them to situations for which they were never intended. For example, some series with little, if any, relationship to movements of the overall economy are often treated as is they are significant predictors of future changes in GNP. Consumer spending in current dollars, discussed in detail in Chapter 4, is one such example. The historical record shows that consumer spending almost always goes up, even when the economy is in recession.

Even so, increases in consumer spending are dutifully reported and widely heralded by the press each time they are released.

Other series are treated as indicators of future overall economic activity when in fact they consistently lag developments in the economy. Interest rates can be cited in this context. For the most part, interest rates tend to follow, rather than lead, changes in the overall economy. Declining interest rates may benefit some sectors of the economy, especially housing, automobiles, and, to some extent, stock prices, but lower interest rates are of little use in predicting future changes in the overall economy.

Yet a third abuse is to focus on nominal dollar values when the real, or inflation-adjusted, figures give a better picture of the underlying changes. Unfortunately, the various government agencies contribute to this problem because the nominal dollar data and the price deflators needed to adjust the data are not available at the same time. When the U.S. Department of Commerce releases its "Advance Monthly Retail Sales" report[4] during the second week of every month, the data is adjusted for seasonal, holiday, and trading-day differences, but not for inflation. By the time inflation-adjusted figures are available, the initial change in retail sales has already been reported and the new figures are of little interest to the media.

A fourth abuse stems from the "creative" use of numbers. For example, a government official may focus on the improvement of a single, and relatively minor, statistic to support the view that the economy is improving when a whole series of other statistics reveals a much bleaker picture. The single most common use of

---

[4] A brief monthly report available on a subscription basis from the Superintendent of Documents, U.S. Government Printing Office, Washington D.C. 20402.

such creative policies it to tell only part of the statistical story, otherwise and more innocently known as "putting one's best foot forward."

Finally, we should note that the media sometimes report on new government figures without giving us enough information to evaluate the significance of the numbers. It is not at all unusual to hear that a particular index went up, say, 4 points, without any mention of the overall level of the index. Four points on a basis of 40 is one thing, but 4 points on an index with a value of 400 may be quite another.

A Final Word

Throughout, the book intends to be ideologically and theoretically neutral. Notice, however, that the economic indicators described in the following six chapters are grouped primarily by economic function, rather than by alphabet or other method. This is to recognize implicitly that while no theoretical or ideological statement is intended, our economy is nevertheless a functioning system made up of identifiable parts that somehow work together.

And remember: we should never become so blinded by the apparent numerical precision and by the "scientific," "theoretical," or "official" nature of these economic indicators that we ignore our own sensitivity to economic and business conditions. This economic awareness, this "feel" for business conditions should be extended to our interpretations of the statistical series as well. We can examine the way statistical series are constructed, and we can look at the historical record to see how they behave. But in the end, it comes down to developing a feel for what they really tell us.

Economic statistics are the tools of the economist and the business forecaster. Like any good tool, they have to be used properly and with care. We hope that this guide will in some small way contribute to a better understanding of the economic statistics that both describe and affect our economic health.

Chapter 2
TOTAL OUTPUT, PRODUCTION, AND GROWTH

Gross National Product

Gross National Product (***GNP***) is formally defined as the market value of all final goods, services, and structures (houses and commercial buildings) produced in one year. As such, it is perhaps *the* most important statistic kept on the economy because it is a measure of total performance. When other economic statistics are used to predict the future of the economy, they are really predicting future changes in GNP.

How Is GNP Measured?

Because GNP is such a comprehensive measure, it is not practical to record every final good, service, or structure produced in the course of one year. Instead, various sampling techniques are used to track subsets of these components so that projections can be made from those samples.

It helps to think of the analysis as being divided into two parts. The first involves a count of the actual number of final goods, services, and structures produced. The second involves assigning a dollar value to the output. If the prevailing market prices are used to value GNP, then the measure is simply *GNP*, or

GNP in current prices. If we want to adjust for the distortions of inflation, we value the output using a set of "base year" prices to get *real GNP*, or *GNP in constant prices.*

Table 2-1 illustrates both types of computation for the U.S. economy in 1988. Suppose that the items in the first column represent actual production in that year. If output is valued at

Table 2-1
Computation of 1988 GNP in Current and Constant Prices

(A) GNP in Current Prices:

Annual Output		Quantity in millions	1988 Prices	Value in millions
Goods:	Automobiles	7	$15,000	$105,000
	Chairs	5	50	250
	........*			
Services:	Legal	8	500	4,000
	Child care	3	700	2,100
	........*			
Structures:	Residential	1.4	120,000	168,000
	Commercial	1	250,000	250,000
	........*			----------
			GNP in Current Dollars	*$4,864,300*

(B) GNP in Constant (1982) Prices:

Annual Output		Quantity in millions	1982 Prices	Value in millions
Goods:	Automobiles	7	$11,000	$77,000
	Chairs	5	40	200
	........*			
Services:	Legal	8	400	3,200
	Child care	3	650	1,950
	........*			
Structures:	Residential	1.4	100,000	140,000
	Commercial	1	220,000	220,000
	........*			----------
			GNP in Constant (1982) Dollars	*$3,996,100*

* Other items in the category

the prices that existed in 1988, the total value of production -- or GNP in current dollars -- amounted to $4,864.3 billion. In the bottom part of the table, the same output is valued at the prices that prevailed in 1982, the base year currently used by the U.S.

Department of Commerce. This measure gives us GNP in constant (1982) dollars of $3,996.1 billion.

The advantage of using constant prices is that it enables us to compare total output in 1988 to total output in 1989, or any other year for that matter. So if real GNP in 1989 grows by 3 percent, the difference *must* be due to changes in the number of goods, services, and/or structures produced. The increase *cannot* be due to inflation, since prices were held constant. The important thing to remember is that, whenever constant prices are used for comparative purposes, only the *percentage change* is relevant, not the constant dollar value of the series.[1]

When Is GNP Reported?

GNP estimates are made quarterly and additional revisions are made as new data becomes available. The Bureau of Economic Analysis (BEA) in the U.S. Department of Commerce releases three estimates according to the following schedule:

Advance -- released in the *first* month after the end of quarter.

Preliminary -- released in the *second* month after the end of quarter.

Final -- released in the *third* month after the end of quarter.

Figure 2-1 below shows the three estimates from the fourth quarter of 1987 through the first quarter of 1989. As you can see, the three estimates for any one quarter are usually fairly close, but they can be off by as much as 1 or 2 percentage points.

---

[1] As long as we focus on percentage changes, the choice of the base year is not important. In fact, base years vary considerably from one series to another: the ***index of industrial production*** uses 1977, ***new private housing permits*** uses 1967, and other series use still other base periods.

Figure 2-1
Quarterly GNP Estimates and Revisions

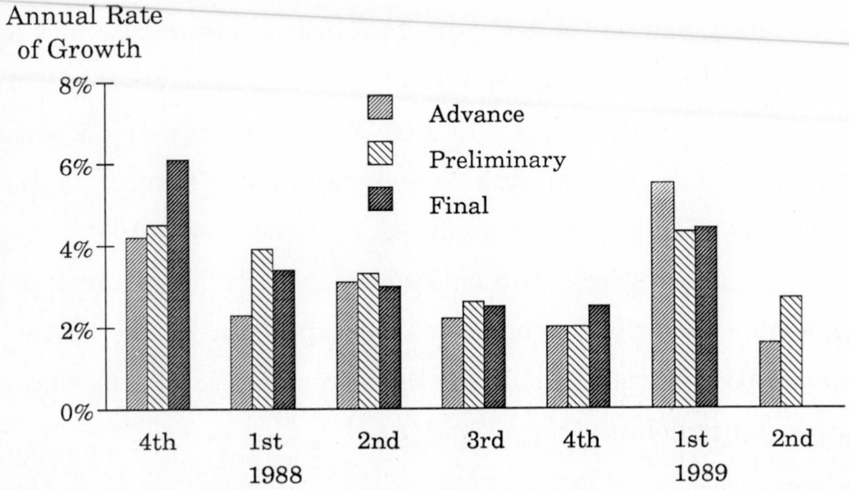

Because of the number of revisions and the delays in getting the estimates, we really don't know how the economy fared during a particular quarter until nearly three months later, and even these estimates are reviewed (and sometimes changed) in July in each of the following three years!

Does GNP Overlook Anything?

You bet! For example, GNP tells us nothing about the *mix* or *composition* of output. A bigger GNP only tells us that the dollar value of total output increased. We don't know if the increase was due to the production of new homes, schools, and libraries or if the production was due to increased production of nerve gas, B-1 bombers, and nuclear weapons.

Also, GNP doesn't tell us anything about the *quality of life*. Depending on your philosophical orientation, you might feel that the quality of life is enhanced every time a city park or museum is built instead of a nuclear reactor.

Perhaps the biggest limitation is that GNP excludes *non-market activities*, such as the services performed by housewives and the services people perform for themselves. For example, GNP will not go up if you mow your own yard, but it will go up if you hire someone else to do it.

Other activities -- prostitution, gambling, and drug running -- are mostly illegal and are simply not reported to the IRS, Department of Commerce, or anyone else. These activities are part of the *underground economy* and are not directly included in GNP, although estimates are made for their inclusion.[2]

When Is the Economy in a Recession?

Historically, a recession occurs whenever real GNP declines for two consecutive quarters. The exact date a recession begins and ends is determined by the National Bureau of Economic Research (NBER), a prestigious private research institute, rather than the U.S. Department of Commerce. This is because of the NBER's long and distinguished record of research into the study and measurement of business cycles.

Since the NBER wants to determine the turning points as accurately as possible, it considers as much data as it can, most of it monthly. As a result, the turning point of an expansion or recession may not always coincide with quarterly changes in real GNP. These reference dates are listed in Table 2-2.

---

[2] In December of 1985, GNP statistics extending back to 1929 were revised upward to account for the unreported activity in the underground economy. As a result of the revision, GNP in 1984 was increased by $119.9 billion. As large as this may seem, many economists in the private sector felt that the revisions were not large enough!

Table 2-2
Business Cycle Expansions and Contractions in the United States

Peak	Trough	Peak	Duration in Months		
			Recession	Expansion	Cycle
June 1857	December 1858	October 1860	18	22	40
October 1860	June 1861	April 1865	8	*46*	*54*
April 1865	December 1867	June 1869	*32*	18	*50*
June 1869	December 1870	October 1873	18	34	52
October 1873	March 1879	March 1882	65	36	101
March 1882	May 1885	March 1887	38	22	60
March 1887	April 1888	July 1890	13	27	40
July 1890	May 1891	January 1893	10	20	30
January 1893	June 1894	December 1895	17	18	35
December 1895	June 1897	June 1899	18	24	42
June 1899	December 1900	September 1902	18	21	39
September 1902	August 1904	May 1907	23	33	56
May 1907	June 1908	January 1910	13	19	32
January 1910	January 1912	January 1913	24	12	36
January 1913	December 1914	August 1918	23	*44*	*67*
August 1918	March 1919	January 1920	*7*	10	*17*
January 1920	July 1921	May 1923	18	22	40
May 1923	July 1924	October 1926	14	27	41
October 1926	November 1927	August 1929	13	21	34
August 1929	March 1933	May 1937	43	50	93
May 1937	June 1938	February 1945	13	*80*	*93*
February 1945	October 1945	November 1948	*8*	37	*45*
November 1948	October 1949	July 1953	11	*45*	*56*
July 1953	May 1954	August 1957	*10*	39	*49*
August 1957	April 1958	April 1960	8	24	32
April 1960	February 1961	December 1969	10	*106*	*116*
December 1969	November 1970	November 1973	*11*	36	*47*
November 1973	March 1975	January 1980	16	58	74
January 1980	July 1980	July 1981	6	12	18
July 1981	November 1982		16		
Averages for Peacetime Cycles Only:					
1857-1982 (25 cycles)			19	27	46*
1857-1919 (14 cycles)			22	24	46*
1919-1945 (5 cycles)			20	26	46*
1945-1982 (6 cycles)			11	34	45*

* Cycles measured peak to peak, trough to trough gives different durations
NOTE: Italicized figures are wartime periods
SOURCE: National Bureau of Economic Research

What About GNP and *Other* Statistics?

Good question! In fact, most of the statistics reported by the various government agencies and reviewed in this book are related to GNP in one way or another. GNP is the measure of *aggregate* economic activity and it can also be broken down into its component parts -- goods, services, business and residential structures, and so on -- for further analysis. Individual statistics can be (and usually are) kept on each of these subcategories.

Some statistics measure the overall performance of a category such as the production of durable goods like motor vehicles and machine tools.[3] Or, the category of durable goods may first be broken down into consumer and business components so that statistics on each component can be compiled. Even other statistics are used to track the production of a particular product like automobiles or residential housing.

The production of GNP also generates profits for business owners as well as wages and salaries for individuals. Since these groups eventually spend their income, more statistics can (and are) kept on expenditures by these groups. Almost every statistic, then, is related to GNP in one way or another.

In Brief

Statistic	*Gross National Product (GNP)*
Compiled by	U.S. Department of Commerce, BEA
Frequency	Quarterly
Release date	End of first month following quarter
Published data	*Survey of Current Business* *Business Conditions Digest*
Hotline update	(202)898-2451 for a 3-5 minute tape message 24 hours a day

[3] Durable goods are generally intended to last more than three years.

Index of Industrial Production

The ***index of industrial production*** is one of several key statistics compiled by the Board of Governors of the Federal Reserve System, or the Fed. The index is compiled monthly and released approximately mid-month of the following month.

Industrial Production and GNP

Earlier, we defined GNP as the market value of all final goods, services, and structures produced in one year. If we break 1988 GNP down into its major components, as in Figure 2-2 below, we can see that the "goods" category amounts to 44.1 percent of the total. The index tracks this component of total output.

Figure 2-2
The Index of Industrial Production and GNP

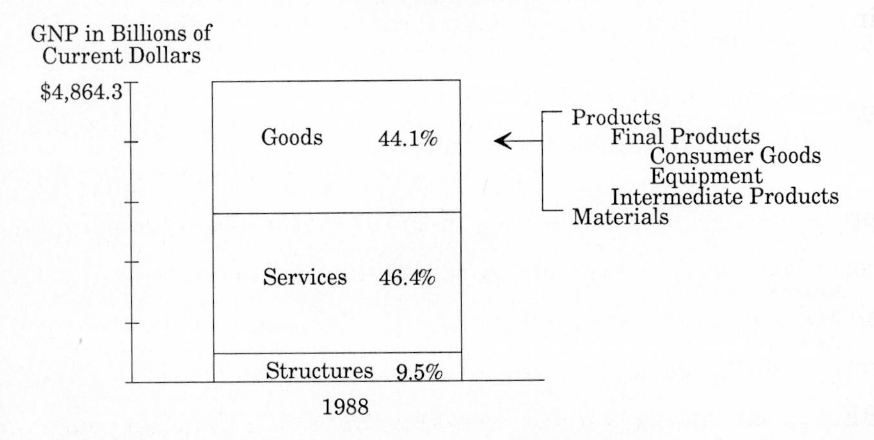

Note that the total industrial production index covers two major categories: products and materials. In addition, the products category is further divided into final and intermediate products, with the former also divided into consumer goods and equipment. Thus, this index is a measure of the goods production activity at all stages of the manufacturing process even though only final products -- not intermediate ones -- are counted in final GNP.

The index and each of its subcomponent series are based on data collected directly from a number of sources, including gas and electric utilities, the Bureau of Mines, the Bureau of the Census, other government agencies, and even industry trade associations. In most cases, the data reflect actual production in the specific industries. In some cases, the Fed even makes an estimate of output based on the number of inputs consumed. In all, approximately 250 individual series of data representing 27 major industries are reflected in the industrial production index.

After the source data are collected, they are compiled and then expressed as a percentage of 1977 output. Of course, the selection of the base year makes little difference since we are interested in the *change* in the index from one month to the next.

What About the Historical Record?

Figure 2-3 on the next page shows that the index of industrial production tends to rise when the economy is expanding and contract when the economy is in recession. This is to be expected, since the production of both durable and nondurable goods represents such a large proportion of overall production. Even the BEA calls the series a coincident one, meaning that the peaks and troughs in the series occur at approximately the same time the economy peaks and troughs.

Figure 2-3
The Index of Industrial Production and Aggregate Economic Activity

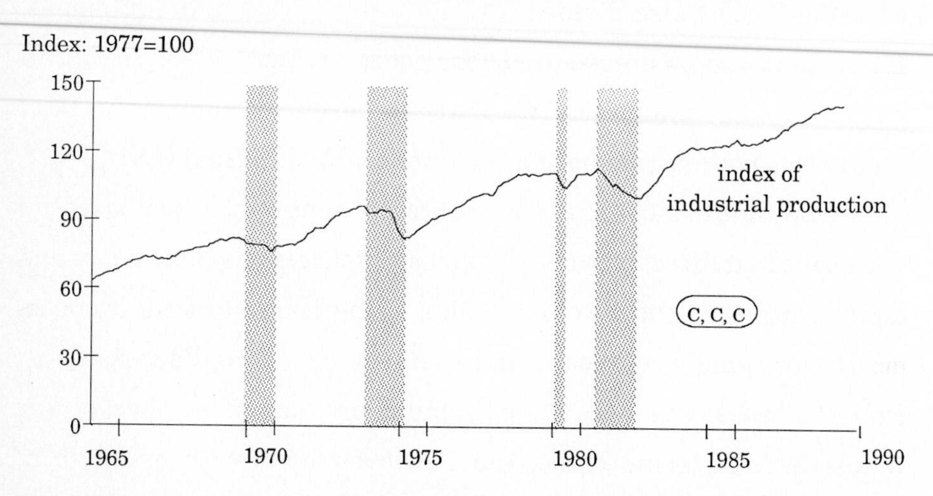

The value of the series is that it gives us a quicker reading on the direction of the total economy than might otherwise be possible. For example, if industrial production (44.1 percent of total GNP in 1988) should drop two percentages points in one month, it stands to reason that total GNP will also be affected. In addition, we are given this information several months before quarterly estimates of GNP and its subsequent monthly revisions are available.

In Brief

Statistic	*The Index of Industrial Production*
Compiled by	The Fed Board of Governors
Frequency	Monthly
Release date	Mid-month on the following month
Published data	Fed Monthly Statistical Release G.12.3 *Federal Reserve Bulletin* *Business Conditions Digest*
Hotline update	None

Durable Goods Production

When the Fed collects data on industrial production, it factors out durable goods as a special category. This series, the ***index of industrial production, durable manufacturers***, is reported monthly and has a base year of 1977. The production of durable goods accounted for 21.5 percent of total GNP in 1988 and will account for a similiar portion in the future..

Are Durable Goods Special?

Yes, for two reasons. First, durable goods are often "big ticket" items. They tend to cost more than most nondurables; they also use a lot of resources as they are produced. Because of this, it is generally thought that the production of durable goods generates more jobs and income than the production of nondurables.

Second, the production of durable goods is very sensitive to changes in the economy since purchasing then can be postponed rather easily. For example, if the economy should weaken, almost anyone can get a few more months out of the old refrigerator, automobile, or whatever. This means that production, and therefore employment, in the durable goods industries may be subject to sudden changes.

As can be seen in Figure 2-4 below, changes in durable goods production are much volatile than nondurables, and they have a tendency to plummet sharply during recessionary periods.

Figure 2-4
Durable and Nondurable Goods Production

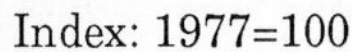

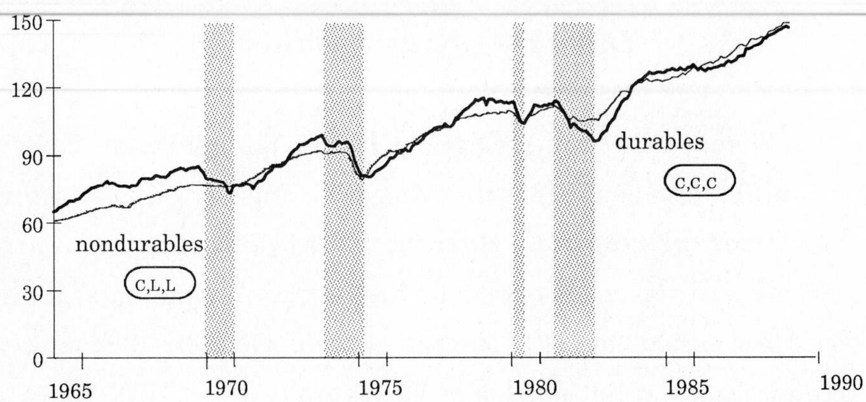

Because of the volatility -- with some monthly changes ranging as high as 3 percent -- and because the index tends to behave as a coincident rather than a leading indicator, even small movements can be a matter of concern.

On the one hand, a drop in the index may indicate that the economy is beginning to enter a recession. On the other hand,[4] the decline may be tempered somewhat by a change in the production of nondurables. For this reason, economists usually look at the overall index to get a better idea of the way the economy is headed.

In Brief

Statistic	*Industrial Production, Durable Manufactures*
Compiled by	The Fed Board of Governors
Frequency	Monthly
Release date	Mid-month on the following month
Published data	Fed Monthly Statistical Release G.12.3 *Federal Reserve Bulletin* *Business Conditions Digest*
Hotline update	None

[4] In order to be absolutely neutral and unbiased, economists should always use two hands.

Building Permits

Residential construction represents a significant component of overall economic activity, amounting to about 4.5 percent of total GNP in 1988. The official title of this series is the ***index of new private housing units authorized by local building permits***, which explains the more common, and considerably shorter, title. This is the most important of several housing series compiled by the Department of Commerce and the only housing series included in the composite *index of eleven leading indicators*.[5]

Do Building Permits Predict Future Economic Activity?

On one level, the relationship between new building permits issued and overall economic activity may seem tenuous. In the first place, a building permit only represents the *intention* to spend rather than a commitment to spend. The permit is also relatively inexpensive to obtain and is sometimes acquired partially for precautionary reasons: "in case" the opportunity to build is right. In addition, the amount of time between issuance of the permit and the beginning (or completion) of the residence may vary greatly from one state, or one residence, to another.

---

[5] Two others are ***new private housing units started***, discussed in the next section, and ***gross private residential fixed investment*** in constant dollars. The latter represents the housing component of the GNP accounts. The Housing and Urban Development (HUD) Department in the Department of Commerce also keeps a series on the sales of new homes. While important, large monthly changes (often in the range of 10 percent) make this a highly volatile series. Even the BEA declines to publish the series in the monthly *Business Conditions Digest*.

Finally, the intent to build may be adversely affected by changes in interest rates after the permit is issued. In short, there are several reasons as to why building permits might not work very well as an economic indicator.

The Historical Record

But work well they do. As can be seen in the figure below, the index of new private housing permits tends to increase sharply during economic expansions and then decline sharply some months before the expansion ends and/or the recession begins. Even before the recession has ended, the index begins to shoot up dramatically, foretelling the impending recovery.

Figure 2-5
Index of New Private Housing Permits

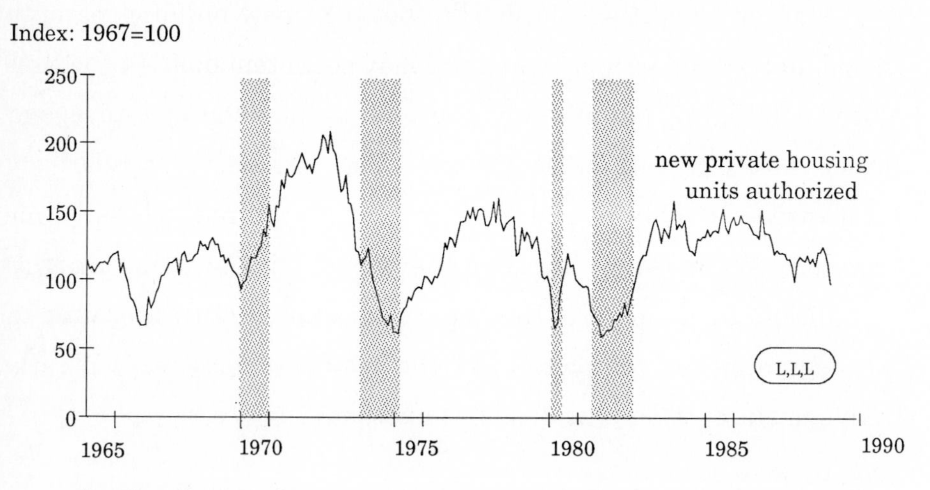

In the figure above, note the size of the swings in the index. The number of permits issued nearly doubled in 1972, when the index reached a high of 206, and then reached a low near 61 (meaning 61 percent of the 1967 level) just three years later in

1975. After the recession of 1981-1982, building permits were up again, but not as dramatically as during the previous decade.

While the index seems to show some volatility over short periods, the chart clearly shows that severe and protracted drops in the index occur just before and sometimes during the early phases of a recession. With the exception of the 1973-1974 recession, the series turned up well before the economy turned up.

For this reason, the index of building permits is classified as a leading indicator and is also included as one of the eleven components of the overall composite *index of leading indicators*.[6]

In Brief

Statistic	*New Private Housing Units Authorized by Local Building Permits*
Compiled by	U.S. Department of Commerce, Bureau of the Census
Frequency	Monthly
Release date	Mid-month for previous month
Published data	*Business Conditions Digest*
Hotline update	None

[6] The preliminary release, on a seasonally adjusted annual basis, is available on the 12th workday of every month and is the one reported in the press. The final figures for the series are available on the 18th and are the ones included in the index of leading indicators.

Housing Starts

Another popular measure of residential construction is the ***new private housing units started*** series.[7] This differs from new building permits in that it represents actual home building activity, not just intention to build.

The Historical Record

The series also differs from the index on building permits in two other important ways. First, it is expressed in terms of millions of private houses started annually, rather than being indexed to a base year. Second, monthly changes in the series are *more* volatile than new building permits:

Figure 2-6
New Private Housing Units Started (annual rate)

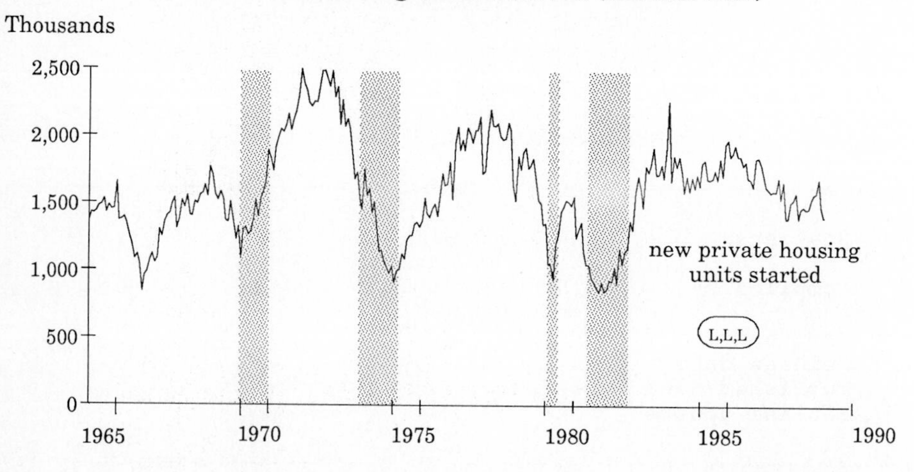

[7] Not to be confused with the ***index of new private housing units authorized by local building permits*** discussed in the previous section.

In fact, it is not uncommon to see the numbers change as much as 10 percent, up or down, in any given month. In January of 1989, housing starts jumped 8 percent and then *dropped* 12.7 percent in February. It turned out that unseasonably warm weather was the culprit. Since builders usually have a backlog of building permits to use, they decided to break ground early when the weather was warm. Because they already had extra units underway when February arrived, the number of starts dropped at that time.

While the Commerce Department adjusts the figures for seasonal variations, they are still revised extensively for several months after they are first released. In addition, the updates frequently include revisions of the *direction* of change as well as the magnitude. As a result, the monthly housing start numbers sometimes seem better suited for commentary and speculation than for forecasting changes in future economic activity.

The main problem is one of interpretation: people seem to focus more on the size of the monthly changes than on the underlying trend and direction of the series. If we ignore the former and focus on the trend, we find that the series behaves fairly well as a leading economic indicator for both peaks and troughs in overall economic activity.

In Brief

Statistic	*New Private Housing Units Started*
Compiled by	U.S. Department of Commerce, Bureau of the Census
Frequency	Monthly
Release date	Third week of the following month
Published data	*Business Conditions Digest*
Hotline update	None

Business Inventories

Historically, inventories have played an important role in the literature on recessions and expansions.[8] In general, high inventories have been singled out as contributing to the cause of recessions, while low inventories are sometimes thought to be a sign that business activity is about to pick up. To see how this might come about, let's take a simplistic look at the process.

How Do Inventory Levels Affect Business Activity?

First, it helps to think of inventories as being residual, in the sense of being "left over," when sales are not up to expectations. Suppose that, for some reason, consumers cut back on their spending. The result is likely to be levels of unsold inventories in excess of what businesses would like to carry. If businesses react by reducing orders from suppliers, closing plants, and/or otherwise cutting back on manufacturing, workers will either work shorter hours or lose their jobs.

This, in turn, reduces the amount of income workers have to spend, which may actually cause inventory levels to *increase* again, rather than decrease, as businesses had planned. If the cycle repeats itself, production will again fall, employment will dip, and

---

[8] W.S. Jevons, Wesley Mitchell and John Maynard Keynes were but a few of the many economists to incorporate the role of inventories into their view of the causes and explanations of economic fluctuations. In the late 1940s, Moses Abramovitz's classic work, The Role of Inventories in Business Cycles, was published by the National Bureau of Economic Research and did much to influence the way inventory statistics are compiled and reported today.

consumer spending will drop, all of which may put the economy on the path to recession.

Eventually, businesses may succeed in reducing production to the point where inventories *are*, in fact, low. If they overshoot their mark, or if consumer spending increases even slightly, inventory shortages may develop. Businesses will then need to hire more, instead of fewer, workers. This increases employment and consumer spending, causing inventories to go down again rather than up. As long as businesses continue to try to replenish inventories, the process of playing catch-up helps pull the economy out of recession and puts it on the path to recovery.

But Does it Really Work Like That?

We can look at the historical record for some clues. In Figure 2-7 below, the level of business inventories is plotted against recent economic activity:

Figure 2-7
The Level of Manufacturing and Trade Inventories

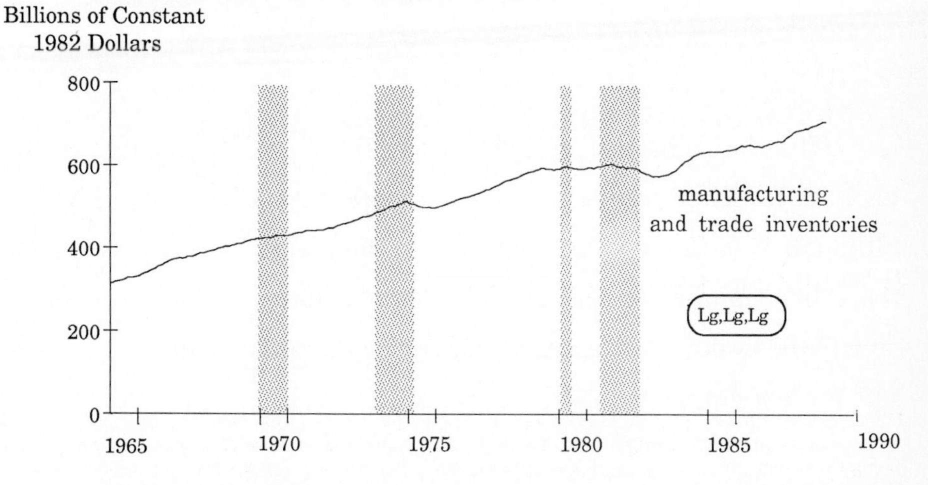

Not very interesting, is it? In fact, most series that report on the *level* of inventories tend to be more of a lagging, not a leading, indicator. This means that inventory levels go up during the expansion and continue to rise right on into the recession. Eventually inventory levels may turn down, but not until the recession is about over.

Let's try again to see if we can do better. This time we will look at the *change* in the level of inventories, rather than at the level itself:[9]

Figure 2-8
The Change in Manufacturing and Trade Inventories

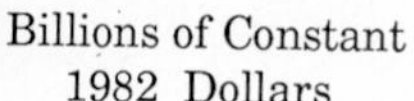

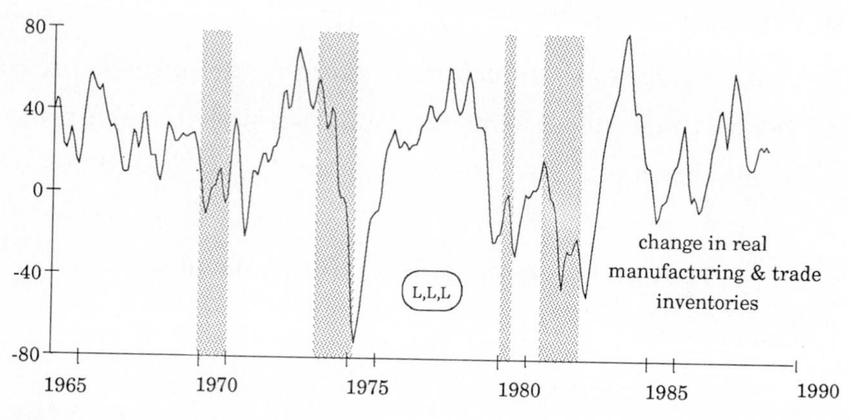

That looks better! According to this series, the change in the level of inventories begins to look more like a leading indicator although it is fairly volatile from one month to the next. That is, the index usually begins to turn down before the economy turns down, and usually turns up before the economy turns up.

---

[9] The data is smoothed using a four-month weighted average with weights of 1,2,2,1 on the last four months. Also, the series used for Figure 2-7 is slightly different from the series used in Figure 2-8 in that the former does not include inventories on order. The difference is relatively minor and has no bearing on the conclusions of the section.

Why Even Bother With Inventory Levels?

Because others do! In fact, a number of financial reporters insist on reporting the level of business inventories, even though they are not helpful as an indicator of *future* economic activity.

One leading financial paper even has a regular monthly feature on the level of manufacturing inventories (a subset of the series used in Figure 2-7). In addition, the report cites the series in current (inflation biased), not constant dollars.[10] As a result, the monthly series usually just goes up.

What Should We Remember About Inventory Statistics?

First, always use a series measured in constant dollars to avoid the distortions caused by inflation. Second, series that track inventory levels are not much help forecasting future economic activity, since they tend to act as lagging indicators. Third, series on changes in the levels tend to act as leading indicators and are most useful for forecasting changes in future economic activity. Finally, if the forecast is for GNP, the choice of which manufacturing or trade inventory series to use is not critical since they all behave about the same.

In Brief

Statistic	*Manufacturing and Trade Inventories in Constant (1982) Dollars*
Compiled by	Bureau of Economic Analysis and Census
Frequency	Monthly
Release date	Second week of following month
Published Data	*Survey of Current Business*
Hotline update	None

[10] Unfortunately, the first release of numbers from any agency in the Department of Commerce is usually on a current dollar basis. This happens because the price index series used to convert current dollars to inflation-adjusted (or real) dollars is not immediately available.

Index of Leading Indicators

One of the most interesting, and occasionally controversial, statistics is the composite ***index of eleven leading indicators***, a monthly series designed to tell us where the economy is headed during the next six to twelve months. Essentially, the series is used as a predictive tool to tell us *if*, and approximately *when*, a recession might take place.

The series is usually released by the Department of Commerce during the last week of every month. It is widely followed and frequently reported in the form of a brief chart such as the one shown in Figure 2-9 below. The index is always current and the latest data are never more than a month old:

Figure 2-9
The Monthly Index of Eleven Leading Indicators

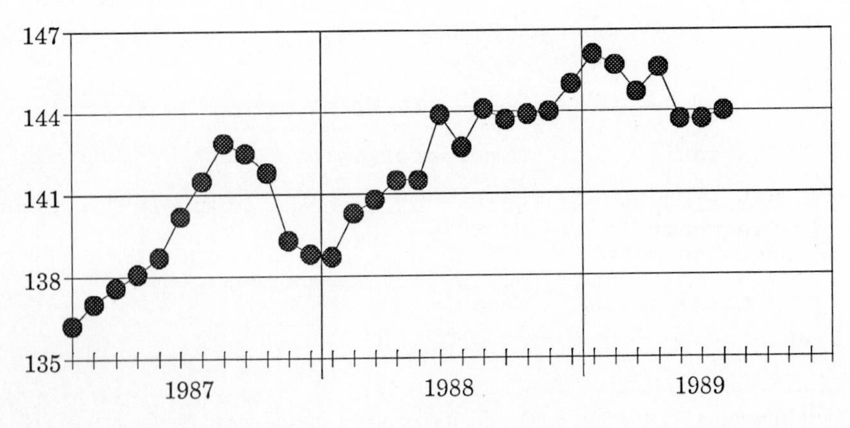

How Do We Interpret the Index?

In general, most observers focus on changes in the direction of the index. For example, if the index should decline for three consecutive months, many believe that the index has "signaled" that a recession is about to begin.

In the same way, three consecutive monthly increases are taken as a sign that the economy will prosper or continue to prosper. The most difficult case to interpret is one where the index goes up one month and then down the next in no particular pattern, essentially the situation encountered in late 1988 and early 1989.

How Was the Index Developed?

Intuitively, the concept of a leading indicator is fairly easy to grasp. We start with the observation that the overall economy is made up of all types of economic activity. Next we ask, could it be that some activities take place or that some events occur in *advance* of changes in the overall economy? If so, perhaps we could focus on these activities and use them to predict how the entire economy might behave in the near future.

Back in the 1950s, the National Bureau of Economic Research thought this might be happening, so they ran thousands of statistical series through their computers and compared the data to changes in real GNP. One set of data examined was an index of stock prices, which (as it turned out) usually declined sharply just before a recession got underway.

Theoretically, the linkage between stock prices and overall spending makes sense. For example, if people feel poorer because of their losses in the market, they might decide to cut back on spending. If enough people feel poorer, their collective decision to spend less may actually affect economic growth.

By itself, however, a measure of stock price performance could not be used as the sole indicator of future economic activity, because stock prices sometimes went down while the economy kept going up. Using the approach that there is safety in numbers, why not look for some other statistical series to combine with stock prices?

It turned out that building permits for private housing also behaved somewhat like stock prices -- the total number of permits issued tended to decrease several months before the economy turned down. Again, this seems to make sense because a decline in building permits may well mean that a substantial amount of economic activity will either be delayed or not take place at all.

Eventually, the list was narrowed down to a handful and combined in the form of a composite index. The resulting series usually changed direction some months *before* the economy did, hence the term *leading* indicator. The index offered considerable promise, so the Department of Commerce took over the task of collecting and publishing the data. The list of component series in the index (the components change from time to time) is presented in Table 2-3 on the next page.

The Historical Record

Most of the controversy concerning the index centers around whether or not three consecutive downturns actually forecast an

Table 2-3
The Index of Leading Indicators, Component Series*

1. Length of average workweek for nonsupervisory workers
2. Average weekly claims for unemployment insurance
3. New manufacturers' orders for consumer goods and materials
4. Vendor deliveries - slower deliveries diffusion index
5. Contracts and orders for plant and equipment
6. New private housing authorized (building permits)
7. Change in manufacturer's unfilled orders
8. Change in sensitive materials prices
9. Stock prices, 500 common stocks
10. Money supply (M2) in 1982 dollars
11. Index of consumer expectations

* As of June 1989

economic slowdown. In Figure 2-10 below, the index of leading indicators has been plotted for a 35-year period beginning in 1965. The shaded areas in the graph represent recessions so that we can compare the turning points of the index to the recessions as they occurred during this period.

Figure 2-10
The Index of Leading Indicators, 1965 to Present

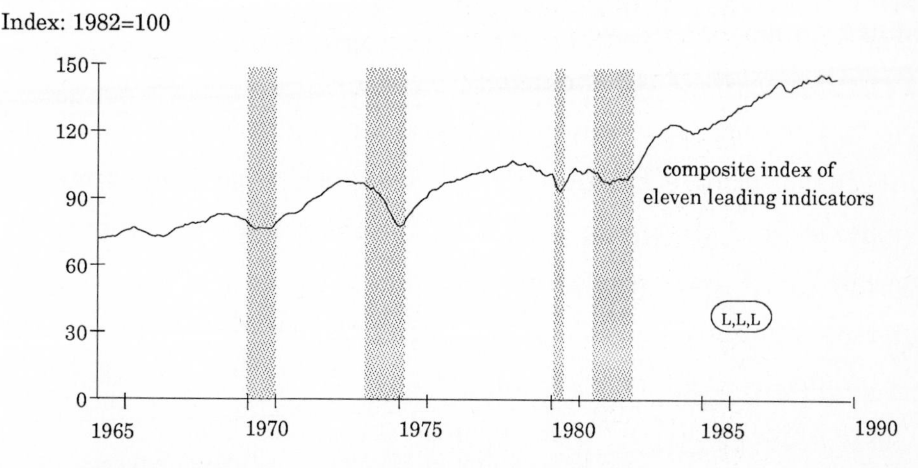

The figure above clearly shows that each recession during this period *was* preceded by a drop in the composite index of leading indicators. The lead time was as much as 15 months in 1978-1979 and as short as 2 months in 1981, with an average lead of 8.25 months.

Less important, but worth mentioning, is the ability of the index to predict when a recession is about to end. According to Figure 2-10, we can see that the lead time is usually one or two months, although there was a 10-month warning in 1982. Since we cannot identify a turning point in the index until at least three months *after* it actually occurs, the economy is usually well out of the recession before it can be predicted by the index.

Has the Index Ever Failed to Predict a Recession?

Yes, on two occasions since 1965, the index predicted a recession that never arrived. The first was in 1966 when the index turned down during each of nine consecutive months starting in April and ending in December. However, heavy (and to some extent hidden) spending on the Vietnam war in the years that followed may well have provided the stimulus needed to avoid the recession predicted by the index.[11]

The second was in 1984 when the index turned down for seven consecutive months. Critics are quick to point out that the index sent a strong signal, yet no recession followed. Advocates argued that massive federal deficit spending, to the tune of $200 billion annually in 1985 and 1986, provided the same type of stimulus as the Vietnam war did earlier. Other than that, the index successfully predicted every recession since 1965.

---

[11] Most economists exclude wartime periods because of the distortion to the domestic statistics. The NBER, for example, compiles separate statistics on the length of peacetime expansions, contractions, and overall business cycles (see Table 2-2).

What About the 5-Month Decline in 1987-1988?

We'll find out soon enough! Since the index declined 5 consecutive months starting in September of 1987 and ending in January of 1988, we should have a pretty good test of the 3-month rule of thumb.

Given the 15-month lead time observed earlier and the inevitable delays in finding out how real GNP actually performed, we'll have to wait until 1989 is almost over to see if the index sent another false signal.

Are There Other Problems with the Index?

Frequent revisions of the monthly numbers are the major source of frustration. For example, there were several periods in 1988 when the index turned down two months in a row. Since many believed that a third consecutive decline usually signals a recession, analysts watched anxiously for next release.

On more than one occasion the new release did show a decline, but the announcement was also coupled with an upward revision of an earlier (negative) number -- leaving us with two newer consecutive months of decline -- and our attention again riveted on the next month's figures.

In Brief

Statistic	*Index of 11 Leading Indicators*
Compiled by	Bureau of Economic Analysis
Frequency	Monthly
Release date	End of following month
Published data	*Business Conditions Digest* *Survey of Current Business*
Hotline update	(202)898-2450 for a brief (3-5) minute recorded message 24 hours a day. The message is updated whenever a component series update is available.

Worker Productivity

The key measure of efficiency in the U.S. economy is worker productivity. The series for all workers is called ***output per hour, all persons, business sector***. It is compiled on a quarterly basis by the Bureau of Labor Statistics and indexed to a base year of 1977=100. The BLS also compiles a second series, ***output per hour, all persons, nonfarm business sector*** which covers manufacturing only.

The Historical Record

The index of worker output per hour, shown in Figure 2-11 below, indicates that the worker productivity has grown slowly but steadily since 1965.

<u>Figure 2-11</u>
Index of Output Per Hour, All Persons, Business Sector

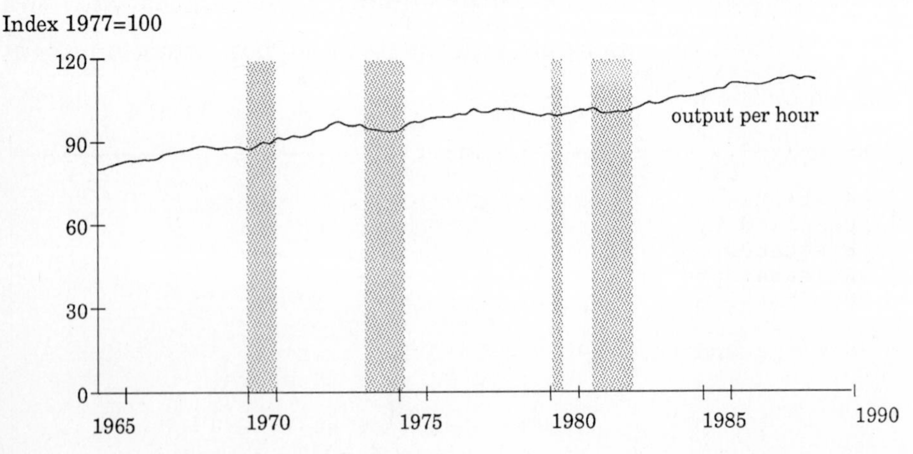

In the first quarter of 1988, the index peaked at 112.8, meaning that workers produced 12.8 percent more output per hour than they did in 1977. When farm workers are removed from the sample, the index slips about a percentage point indicating slightly lower productivity in manufacturing.

Is Worker Productivity a Useful Economic Indicator?

Worker productivity is of little use as an indicator of future economic activity for two reasons. First, the series is based on quarterly data which is not especially well suited to forecasting turning points in economic activity.

Second, neither the level of the series nor changes in the level (remember the discussion on inventories?) exhibit the type of stable and predictable movement that can be related to overall economic activity. Even Figure 2-11 above reveals that worker productivity sometimes goes up during recessions.

However, the series is extremely useful if we want to examine or explain some of the factors that contribute to long-term economic growth. Worker productivity is a long-term trend measure and should be evaluated from this perspective.[12]

In Brief

Statistic	*Output Per Hour, All Persons, Business Sector*
Compiled by	Bureau of Labor Statistics
Frequency	Quarterly
Release date	Four to five weeks after close of quarter
Published data	*Business Conditions Digest*
Hotline update	None

---

[12] The BLS compiles several other productivity measures, but only the ones discussed here are published regularly by the BEA in *Business Conditions Digest*. See Chapter 10, "Productivity Measures: Business Sector Productivity and Major Subsectors," in the *BLS Handbook of Methods*, April 1988, for other measures.

Capacity Utilization

When the Federal Reserve System collects data on industrial production, it also makes estimates of manufacturing capacity. The ***capacity utilization rate, manufacturing*** is the ratio of industrial production to capacity. Estimates of industrial capacity are available for a number of industries and product groups, including manufacturing, mining, utilities, durable goods, chemicals, and paper, to name a few. The monthly series is released approximately two weeks after the close of the month.

Why Is Capacity Important to the Fed?

One of the responsibilities of the Fed is to foster steady economic growth in a climate of reasonable price stability. The capacity utilization rate is designed to tell the Fed if the economy is "heating up" to the point where inflation might surge because of bottlenecks in production. This sometimes happens when demand for output is so strong that producers are tempted to use less skilled labor and less efficient equipment to generate even more output.

This makes the series a little different in that it is not exclusively intended to forecast changes in future economic activity. Instead, the series is designed as a guide to monetary policy. When the capacity utilization rate gets too high, the Fed might be tempted to tighten the money supply to slow the economy and lessen the potential threat of inflation.

What About the Historical Record?

The overall capacity utilization rate for manufacturing, expressed in percentage terms, is shown in Figure 2-12 below. Since it is expressed as a percent of capacity, the level never exceeds 100 percent.

Figure 2-12
Capacity Utilization Rate, Manufacturing

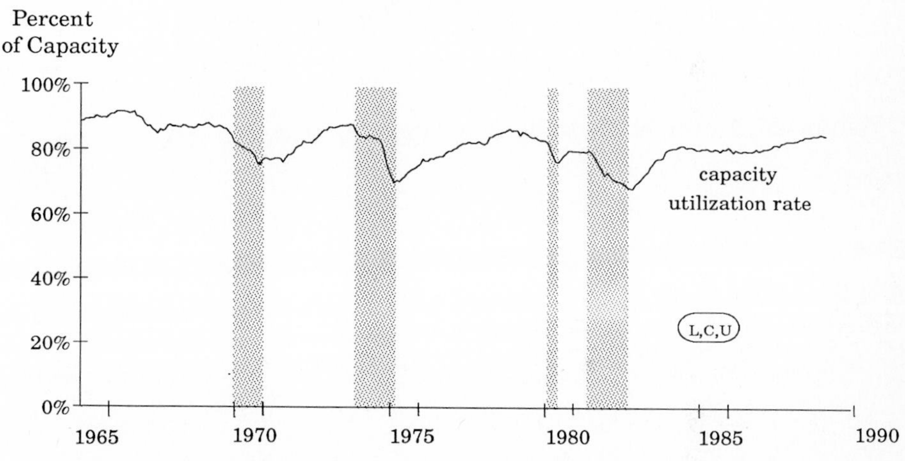

Even though the series was not intended to be an indicator of future economic activity, it still tends to peak several months before the economy peaks. Unfortunately, the lead time is too unpredictable to be of much value for forecasting purposes. Because of these characteristics, the BEA gives the series an overall rating of "unclassified" as a cyclical indicator.

In Brief

Statistic	*Capacity Utilization Rate, Manufacturing*
Compiled by	The Fed Board of Governors
Frequency	Monthly
Release date	Mid-month in the following month
Published data	Statistical Release G.3(402)
	Federal Reserve Bulletin
	Business Conditions Digest
Hotline update	None

Chapter 3
EMPLOYMENT, INCOME, AND EARNINGS

The Unemployment Rate

Unemployment numbers, specifically the ***civilian unemployment rate***, or simply the ***unemployment rate***, are among the most widely watched of all economic statistics. The rate can move as much as one or two percentage points in a short period of time, but it has been contained to a much smaller range since the great depression of the 1930s, when it peaked at nearly 25 percent.

Figure 3-1
The Monthly Unemployment Rate

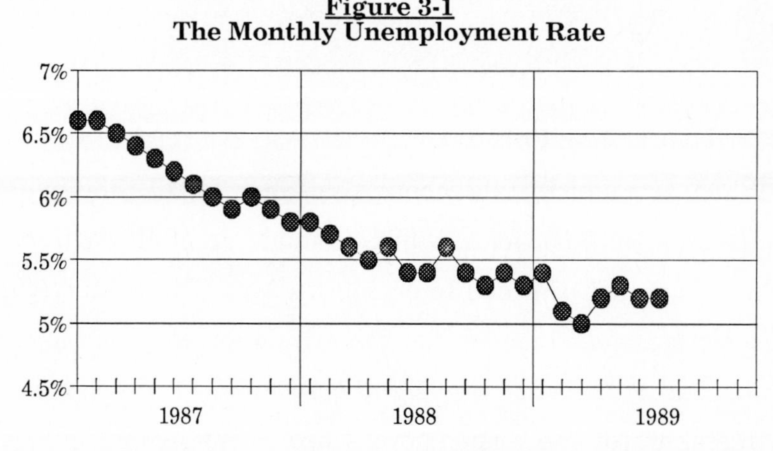

Even so, monthly movements as small as one-tenth of one percent are usually regarded as fairly important and are widely reported by the press. As we shall see, the attention is generally warranted, so let's take a closer look to see how the data are collected and what they really mean.

How Are the Data Collected?

Unemployment data are collected monthly by the Bureau of the Census for the Bureau of Labor Statistics (BLS) using a survey covering approximately 55,800 households in 1,973 counties and independent cities, with coverage in all 50 states and the District of Columbia. For consistency, the survey covers the week containing the 12th day of the month. The BLS usually releases the unemployment numbers during the first full week of the following month. For example, the unemployment figures in the illustration above were released on Friday, July 7, 1989.

Employment surveys are designed to classify people into one of three groups: employed, unemployed, or not in the labor force. The data are then broken down according to marital status, age, sex and race. If a person has more than one job, only the one requiring the *most* hours per week is counted and the other is ignored.

The Civilian Labor Force

When economists talk about the labor force, they generally mean the *civilian labor force*, which is made up of all civilians over 16 years of age not confined to an institution. The term *civilian* is used to separate out members of the armed forces, who make up a small (under 2 percent) but significant part of the labor force. Since members of the armed forces are always considered to be employed (see the definition below) the unemployment rate would tend to go down if we included several million people who all had jobs!

The part of the definition concerning the noninstitutional population is also intended to exclude those confined to a mental hospital or prison. After all, they can hardly be expected to be able to go out and seek, let alone hold, a job. Finally, the age limitation means that an enterprising 15 year old working 50 hours a week cannot be counted as either being employed or unemployed: the person is simply outside the definition of the labor force.

Are You Employed?

We can find out. Suppose, for example, that you were interviewed by the Census Bureau during March 1989.[1] Basically, you would have been asked the following questions (remember that the 12th of the month falls on a Sunday so the relevant week is the 12th through the 18th:)

> "During the week of the 12th through the 18th,
>
> 1. Did you work at least <u>one</u> hour for pay or profit?
> 2. Did you work more than 15 hours for <u>no pay</u> in a family business?
> 3. Did you have a job or business, but did not to report because of illness, weather, labor disputes, vacation, or other personal reasons?"

If you answered "yes" to *any* one of the questions above, then you would have been classified as employed!

Who Are the Unemployed?

Good question. After all, if someone can be defined as employed by working as little as one hour during the survey week, what does it take to be unemployed? Let's assume that our

---

[1] We chose this month for illustration because unemployment had not been this low since January 1974, a span of more than 15 years.

respondent answered "no" to all of the questions above. Now two more criteria have to be met, so we ask:

4. Did you make specific efforts to find a job during the past month? (Note: Efforts to find a job range from a formal application to simply checking with friends.)

5. Were you available for work this week (the week of the 12th through the 18th)?

If the answer to both questions is "yes," the person would be considered unemployed.[2]

Have We Accounted for Everyone?

Not quite. Suppose, for example, that someone answered "no" to our first three questions. From this, we know that they are not employed. However, if they fail to answer "yes" to both of the next two questions, they cannot be considered unemployed either. What is their classification status?

These people are simply defined as dropouts or not officially part of the labor force. In reality, dropouts are fairly common. Some people become so discouraged that they stop looking for a job. To avoid being a dropout, people have to make an effort, even a meager one, to find work *and* to be available at the same time. During periods of recession or in areas where the number of homeless is quite high, the number of dropouts can be significant.

How Do We Get the Unemployment Rate?

This is the easy part. After we determine the number of unemployed persons, we divide them by the size of the civilian labor force. In March 1989, the numbers looked like this:

---

[2] Individuals on temporary layoff from another job or waiting to report to a new job within the next 30 days do *not* need to be looking for employment to be considered unemployed.

$$\text{Unemployment rate} = \frac{\text{number unemployed}}{\text{civilian labor force}} = \frac{6.1 \text{ million}}{123.2 \text{ million}} = 5.0\%$$

By the way, since we divided the total number of unemployed persons by the civilian labor force, we really have the *civilian* unemployment rate, the most common measure of overall unemployment. Since the monthly survey data also identifies the unemployed by sex, race, age, and marital status, we could also get the unemployment rate for adult men, adult women, all teenagers, whites, blacks, black teenagers, and Hispanics. Unemployment rates for these groups are frequently reported along with the overall civilian unemployment rate discussed above.

Are Unemployment Numbers Really Significant?

More than you might imagine! Even a relatively small change in the monthly unemployment rate involves a large number of people. For example, with a civilian labor force of 123.3 million, an increase in the unemployment rate of just one-tenth of one percent would mean that an additional 123,300 individuals would be out of work. This is more than the total number of people currently living in Albany, New York or San Bernardino, California!

Finally, we should point out that the unemployment rate in the United States is generally higher than those reported in many European countries, a difference due primarily to the way the statistics are compiled. In the United States, we make an effort to *look* for the unemployed. In most other countries, people are not even counted as being unemployed until they actually show up to collect an unemployment check. If people in these countries have an aversion to being on welfare, and if they do not make an effort to claim unemployment checks, the unemployment rate will be understated even though these same people might be unemployed by our standards.

What About the Historical Record?

Today most economists would agree that an unemployment rate in the vicinity of 5 percent is relatively low. As can be seen in Figure 3-2 below, 5 percent is relatively low for the period of the 1980s, but there have been other periods when it was even lower. One of the more interesting things, however, is that the unemployment rate tends to vary considerably with the state of the economy.

Figure 3-2
The Civilian Unemployment Rate and the Business Cycle

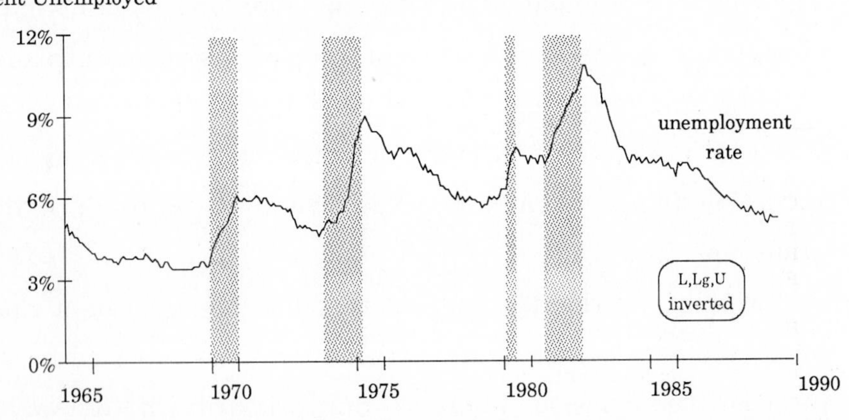

For example, whenever the economy is in a state of expansion (represented by the unshaded areas in Figure 3-2), the unemployment rate tends to fall -- and somewhat slowly at that.

However, when the economy is in a state of recession (represented by the shaded areas), the unemployment rate moves up fairly rapidly. Indeed, one of the major concerns of economists is the speed at which the unemployment rate can climb.

While the more recent unemployment numbers in Figure 3-1 on page 47 look good, we should be realize that (1) they are not especially low from a historical viewpoint and (2) that they are subject to sudden change.

Aside from the pain, suffering, and sheer waste of resources represented by the index, the unemployment rate has some value as an indicator of future economic activity. Although the warning period is relatively short, the series tends to be a leading indicator of future economic downturns and a lagging indicator of impending recoveries.[3] However, the rate lags the recovery, which limits its overall value as a general indicator.

In Brief

Statistic	*Civilian Unemployment Rate*
Compiled by	Bureau of Labor Statistics
Frequency	Monthly
Release date	First week of following month
Published data	*Employment and Earnings* *Business Conditions Digest*
Hotline update	(202)523-9658 for a 4-minute update on consumer prices, producer prices and the unemployment rate

[3] The BEA inverts, or turns the series "upside down," for classification purposes (the series is not inverted in Figure 3-2). The adjustment is made for the sake of appearances only. When the series is inverted, it looks more like others we have observed which turn down before the economy turns down. New jobless claims, discussed on page 54, are also inverted for the same reasons.

New Jobless Claims

The Employment and Training Administration in the U.S. Department of Labor maintains another cyclical indicator of employment and overall economic activity: the ***average weekly initial claims for unemployment insurance, state programs*** series, more commonly known as "new jobless claims." Since these claims are made at the state level, the ETA collects this information from state agencies.

The Historical Record

In the figure below, new jobless claims are plotted against aggregate economic activity.[4] The vertical scale is in thousands,

Figure 3-3
New Jobless Claims

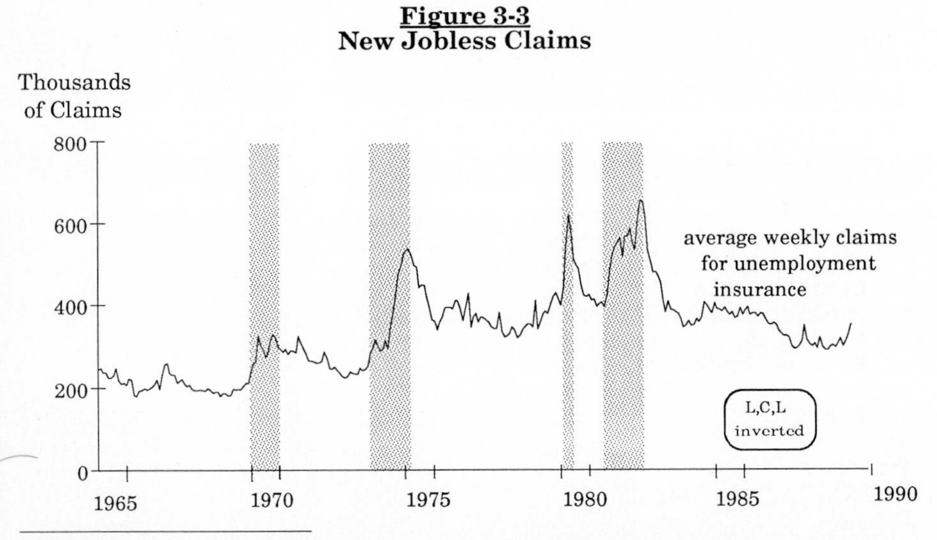

[4] The ETA releases weekly figures as they become available, usually at the end of the second week following the reporting period. The weekly data is converted to a monthly basis and forwarded to BEA for publication in *Business Conditions Digest*. The historical data for the series is kept in monthly form and is the one used in Figure 3-3.

with recent unemployment claims usually numbering between 300,000 and 400,000.

Are New Jobless Claims an Economic Indicator?

Since labor is a variable cost, meaning that the number of workers employed usually varies with changes in the level of production, new claims for unemployment insurance are intuitively appealing as an economic indicator.

Indeed, Figure 3-3 shows that new claims tend to decline during expansionary periods and then rise several months before the recession actually begins. According to the Bureau of Economic Analysis in the Department of Commerce, the series is a leading indicator when it comes to forecasting peaks in economic activity, a coincident indicator when it comes to predicting when the economy will bottom out, and a leading indicator overall.[5]

However, since the lead times for both the peaks and the troughs are fairly uniform, the Bureau of Economic Analysis has given the series an overall "leading indicator" classification.

In Brief

Statistic	*Average Weekly Initial Claims for Unemployment Insurance, State Programs*
Compiled by	Education and Training Administration, U.S. Department of Labor
Frequency	Weekly
Release date	Second week following close of latest reporting week
Published data	*Business Conditions Digest*, monthly *Unemployment Insurance Claims*, weekly bulletin, ETA, Department of Labor
Hotline update	(202)535-0888

[5] This series, like the unemployment rate shown in Figure 3-2 is inverted for classification purposes.

New Jobs Created

One so-called statistic is ***new jobs created***, usually stated in terms of number of jobs created during the month -- or, in even-numbered years, since the last election. Despite its widespread reputation, "new jobs created" is not a statistic at all. Neither the federal government nor any other group compiles this statistic.

The reason is that limitations inherent in the source data makes the series difficult to compile on a reliable basis. For example, BLS estimates total employment from two data sources: a survey of business establishments and a survey of households conducted by the Bureau of the Census. The problem is that the total number of people employed, as reported by each survey, hardly ever matches because of multiple jobholders!

Suppose you worked 20 hours at a department store and 17 at McBurger's. The business survey would reveal two jobs, but the household survey would find only one person employed. To reconcile the difference, the BLS simply *combines* the two and records one person as being employed 37 hours at the establishment where the most hours are worked.

Because of growth in the number of *part-time* jobs, total employment as measured by the survey of business establishments usually grows faster than the household survey. Growth in the establishment series is usually -- and mistakenly -- cited as the source of the new jobs created "statistic."

Personal Income

Personal income sounds as if it should be about the income people earn: their salaries, tips, and hourly wages. In a way it is, but in a more fundamental sense, ***personal income*** represents the total current income received by persons from all sources, *minus* contributions to social insurance. As such, we think of personal income as one of the major components of GNP.

Personal Income and GNP

We can explain the derivation of personal income using the actual numbers for GNP in 1988.

Let's start with GNP in current dollars of $4,864.3 billion. Next, subtract the wear and tear on the capital stock, more formally known as capital consumption allowances, to get *net national product* (*NNP*) of $4,357.9 billion. The government sector then takes a slice of the income earned by businesses in the form of indirect business taxes,[6] and the remainder, called *national income* (*NI*), is $3,968.2 billion. This represents the sum of employee compensation, proprietor's income, rental income, corporate profits, and net interest payments in the economy.

Several final adjustments, shown in Figure 3-4, are needed to get personal income. The income kept by the business sector, known as retained earnings or undistributed corporate profits, are subtracted. So are social insurance payments like social security.

---

[6] Licenses, taxes, and other fees a firm pays in order to do business.

Figure 3-4
The Derivation of Personal Income from GNP*

Billions of
Current Dollars

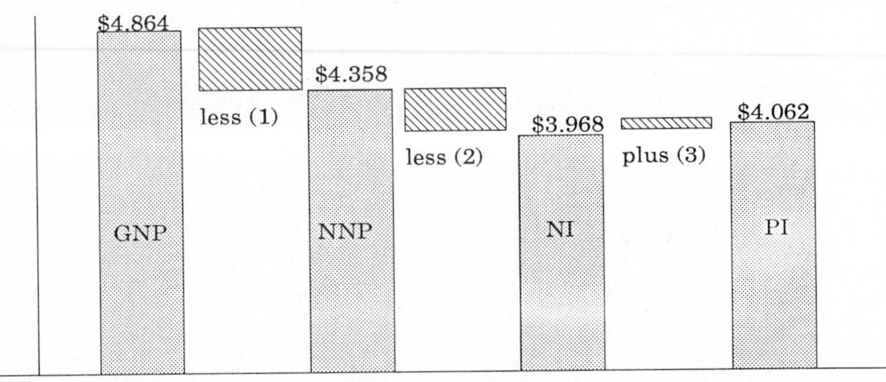

* data is for 1988
(1) CCA is subtracted to get net national product (NNP)
(2) Indirect business taxes are subtracted to get national income (NI)
(3) Undistributed corporate profits and social insurance payments are subtracted, and transfer payments are added to get personal income (PI)

Finally, transfer payments, such as unemployment compensation, welfare, and aid to families with dependent children, are added in. The result is the aggregate measure called *personal income* (*PI*) in the amount of $4,062.1 billion.

Now That We Have It, What Can We Do With It?

Plot it, naturally, and see what it looks like.

In Figure 3-5, the level of personal income is plotted against the familiar backdrop of business expansions and contractions. Even when measured in constant dollars, the overall trend seems to be up during expansions and a little flat to negative during recessions. In fact, personal income might have been down a little more during the recessionary periods if it were not for transfer payments which act as buffers to cushion the decline in income.

In retrospect, this is exactly the pattern we should have expected. Personal income is such a large component of GNP, approximately 84 percent, that both *should* go up and down together, even though the movements are relatively small.

Figure 3-5
Personal Income in Current and Constant Dollars

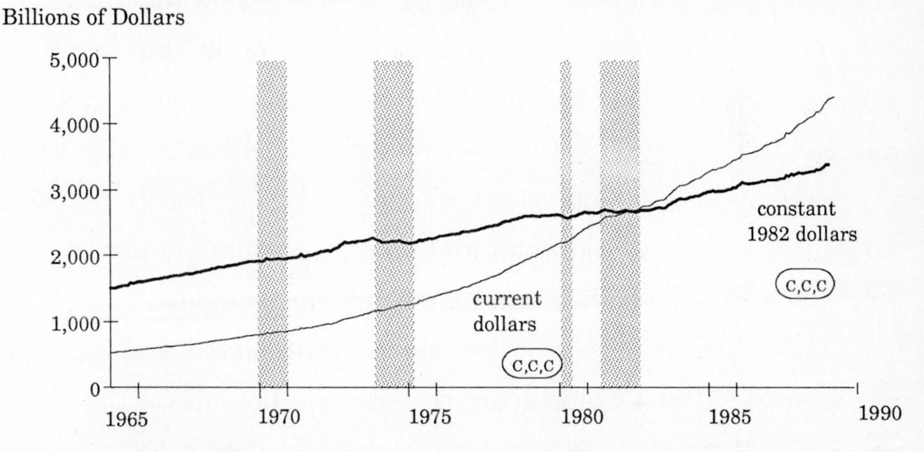

Even its official status with the Bureau of Economic Analysis is that of a coincident, rather than a leading, indicator.

Are Coincident Indicators Useful Indicators?

Of course! They tell us where we are and how we are doing. They just don't give us *advance* warning of where the economy is heading as do changes in leading indicators.

The value of personal income is that it is computed more frequently than GNP, monthly rather than quarterly, so we don't have to wait so long to find out how the economy is doing. In essence, think of personal income as a *proxy* for current economic activity, even though the official report on GNP may not be available for some time.

Is There Anything It Doesn't Tell Us?

It tells us very little about the distribution of income. Like GNP, it is such a comprehensive measure that we cannot tell how it is divided among those who receive it. It is entirely possible (although unlikely) that most of the increases in personal income go only to the very wealthy. Of course, the increases could go to minimum wage recipients instead, but we don't know that either.

One other thing we should be aware of is that monthly releases of personal income (and disposable personal income discussed in the next section) are reported in *current*, rather than in constant (inflation-adjusted), dollars. The reason is that the numbers needed to make the inflation adjustments are usually not available when the personal income figures are compiled.

As a result, current dollar figures are released and reported in the press. This is unfortunate because inflation makes the series appear to grow even faster than it actually does. Even if real personal income is flat, inflation will make it appear as if it is rising.

In Brief

Statistic	*Personal Income*
Compiled by	U.S. Department of Commerce, BEA
Frequency	Monthly
Release date	End of month for previous month
Published data	*Survey of Current Business* *Business Conditions Digest*
Hotline update	(202)898-2452 for a 3-5 minute recorded message

Disposable Personal Income

Another widely followed measure is ***disposable personal income*** (***DPI***), the income available to persons for spending and saving. It is also part of the GNP statistics and is compiled and released by the Department of Commerce on a monthly basis.[7]

Deriving Disposable Personal Income

Disposable income is derived by subtracting personal taxes and nontax payments from the personal income that was shown in Figure 3-4. DPI is shown in Figure 3-6 below:

Figure 3-6
Disposable Personal Income and GNP*

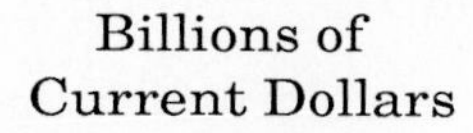

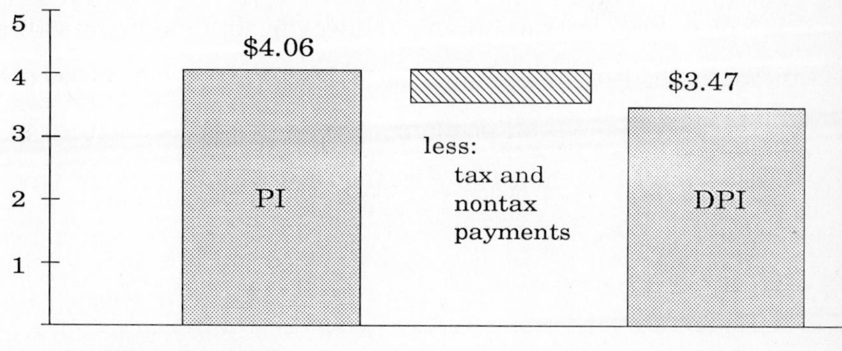

* data for 1988

Like personal income, disposable personal income is relatively large, accounting for approximately 71 percent of GNP.

---

[7] Like the statistics on ***personal income***, the preliminary release is usually in terms of current (inflation biased) dollars.

Does It Have Value as an Economic Indicator?

It would seem so, because disposable personal income is the income people actually have left over for spending purposes. The historical record for the series is presented in Figure 3-7 below:

Figure 3-7
Disposable Personal Income in Current and Constant Dollars

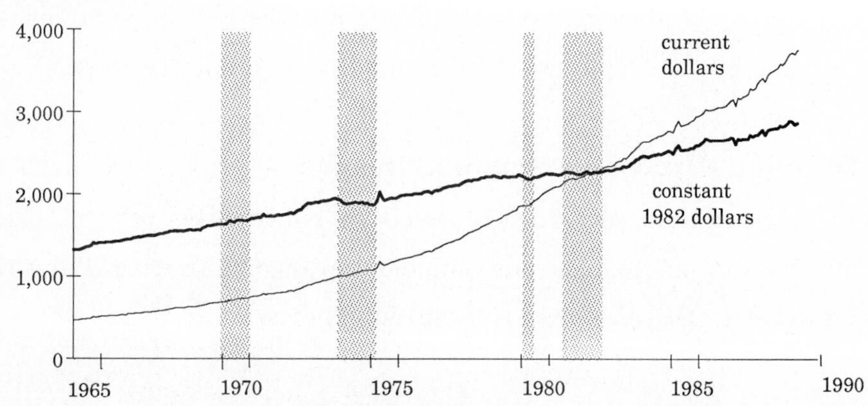

The series is designed to track the income the consumer sector has available to spend and is therefore a valuable indicator of our economic well-being. However, it has little value as an indicator of future economic activity since it varies so little with changes in the overall economy. Even the BEA declines to classify it as a cyclical indicator, listing it instead under the general heading of "other important economic measures."

In Brief

Statistic	*Disposable Personal Income (DPI)*
Compiled by	U.S. Department of Commerce, BEA
Frequency	Monthly
Release date	End of month for previous month
Published data	*Survey of Current Business* *Business Conditions Digest*
Hotline update	(202)898-2452 for a 3-5 minute message

Help-Wanted Advertising

One of the few major statistics collected by a non-governmental agency is the index of ***help-wanted advertising in newspapers***. The monthly index is compiled by The Conference Board and is available from 1960 to the present with 1967 used as the base year.

How Is the Index Compiled?

The Conference Board collects data on the number of help-wanted classified ads printed in 51 cities around the country. In each city, a count of all classified ads is taken from a single newspaper, and the total is adjusted for both seasonal patterns and the number of days in each calendar month.[8] The count for each city is then weighted according to the size of the labor market in the region and, after some other minor adjustments, compiled and released.

What About Its Value as an Indicator?

The monthly help-wanted index is plotted against the recent series of business expansions and contractions in Figure 3-8 on the next page. As the illustration shows, the index peaks several months before the expansion ends. It then continues to fall during the recession and does not recover until or after the expansion actually begins.

---

[8] See *The Help-Wanted Index: Technical Description and Behavioral Trends*, Conference Board Report No. 716.

Figure 3-8
Help-Wanted Advertising in Newspapers

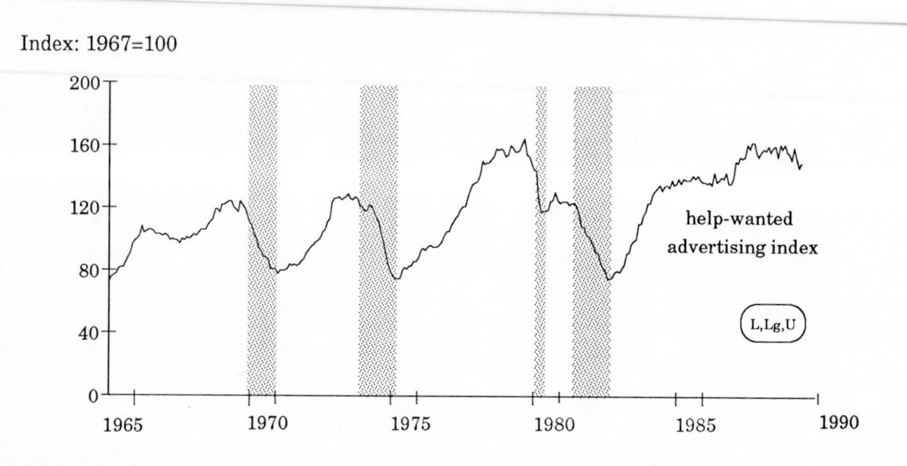

The reliability of the index is such that it is also reported by the BEA in its monthly edition of *Business Conditions Digest*. The BEA classifies the index as a leading indicator for recessions and a lagging indicator for recoveries. This means that the series has an overall rating as "unclassified," but that does not diminish its value as a tool for predicting when the next recession might arrive.

In Brief

Statistic	*Help-Wanted Advertising in Newspapers*
Compiled by	The Conference Board 845 Third Avenue New York, NY 10022
Frequency	Monthly
Release date	First week of following month
Published data	Conference Board Report No. 716 *Business Conditions Digest*
Hotline update	None

Chapter 4
SALES, SPENDING, AND PROFITS

Consumer Spending

The overall spending activity by consumers is often considered to be an indicator of the economy's health. Consumer spending is monitored by the U.S. Department of Commerce and is reported on a monthly basis in both current and constant (1982) dollars.

However, if you look in the Department of Commerce's index to current statistics, you won't find it listed under "consumer" or even "spending." Instead, it is called ***personal consumption expenditures*** and is listed in the *disposition of personal income* tables.

How Is Consumer Spending Related to GNP?

To understand how the two are tied together, it helps to think of the economy as being divided into "sectors." The consumer sector is the largest, followed by the government, business, and foreign sectors.

The total income generated by the production of GNP is called *national income*, and the portion received by the consumer sector is called *personal income.*[1] Consumers pay taxes on personal income, and the amount left over is called *disposable personal income.* This in turn can either be spent on goods and services, paid out as interest, transferred to foreigners, or retained in the form of personal saving.[2] These relationships are illustrated in Table 4-1:

Table 4-1
Consumer Spending and the Disposition of Personal Income in 1988, Billions of Current Dollars

Personal Income			$4,062.1
less: Personal tax and nontax payments			590.3
Disposable Personal Income			3,471.8
less: Personal outlays			
Personal Consumption Expenditures		***3,227.5***	
Durable goods	451.1		
Nondurable goods	1,046.9		
Services	1,729.6		
Interest paid by consumers to business		98.9	
Personal transfer payments to foreigners		1.0	
Total personal outlays			3,327.5
Personal Saving			$144.7

The personal consumption expenditure component of total personal outlays, amounting to $3,227.5 billion, is generally referred to as *consumer spending.*

How Does Consumer Spending Behave Over Time?

As can be seen in Figure 4-1 below, the series on personal consumption expenditures is remarkably steady. The monthly data shows some slight variations, but consumer spending generally tends to go up, regardless of whether the economy is expanding or not.

1 The derivation of **personal income (PI)** and **disposable personal income (DPI)** was explained earlier in Chapter 3. You may want to review these sections for additional background on the national income and product accounts.
2 Students of economics will immediately recognize the Keynesian proposition that consumers either save or consume their income.

Figure 4-1
Consumer Spending and Aggregate Economic Activity

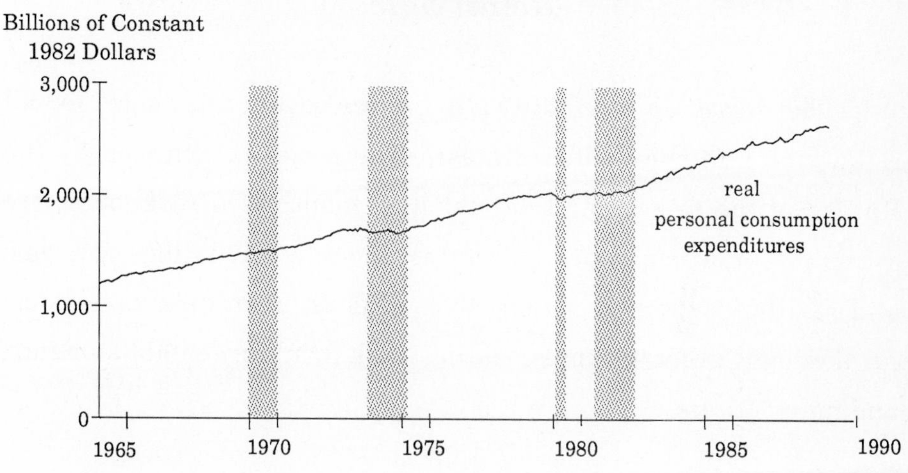

The personal consumption expenditures series is important for two reasons: it gives us an idea of what is happening in the consumer sector and it is useful for tracking long-run trends. However, it does not exhibit the type of behavior that allows us to predict changes in future economic activity.

Expenditures on durables, nondurables, and services are also available with the release of the personal consumption expenditure series. Since the report is available later in the month, constant dollar estimates such as those used in the figure above are usually provided.

In Brief

Statistic	*Personal Consumption Expenditures* (known informally as *Consumer Spending*)
Compiled by	U.S. Department of Commerce, BEA
Frequency	Monthly
Release date	Last week in month for previous month
Published data	*Survey of Current Business*
Hotline update	(202)898-2452 for updates of quarterly and monthly personal income figures

Retail Sales

The series on ***monthly retail sales*** covers total sales for all retail stores in the United States. The series is compiled by the Bureau of the Census and is published monthly. Breakdowns are available for a variety of industries, including building materials and hardware stores, automotive dealers, furniture and home furnishings, grocery stores, eating and drinking establishments, and many others.

The Historical Record

The initial release of monthly retail sales data is not adjusted for inflation, although adjusted data is available shortly thereafter. For purposes of comparison, both series are plotted in Figure 4-2 below:

Figure 4-2
Retail Sales and Aggregate Economic Activity

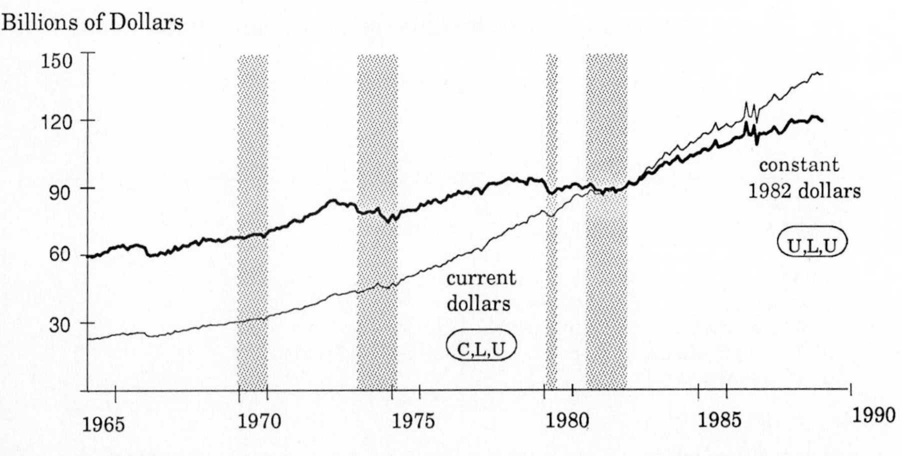

For the most part, sales in retail stores are made to the consumer sector whose spending patterns are remarkably stable. Because of this, we might expect that total retail sales behave much the same. Indeed, Figure 4-2 confirms this suspicion.

How Does It Fare as an Indicator?

When retail sales are measured in terms of current dollars, the series almost always goes up, even during recessionary periods. As a result, the series won't tell us if a recession is either underway or about to begin.

When the series is adjusted for inflation by expressing it in terms of constant 1982 dollars, it tends to peak before the economy peaks, although the lead time is variable. Again, the series -- even when adjusted for inflation -- won't help predict a recession.

If the economy is in a recession, however, and if we are trying to predict when the recession might end, the series on total retail sales might be helpful. In fact, the series -- whether measured in current or constant dollars -- tends to recover before the economy recovers, making it a *leading indicator* for recoveries.

In Brief

Statistic	*Monthly Retail Sales*
Compiled by	Bureau of the Census, Department of Commerce
Frequency	Monthly
Release date	Two weeks after the close of the month
Published data	*Business Conditions Digest* *Monthly Retail Trade, Sales and Inventories,* a Current Business Report from the U.S. Department of Commerce
Hotline update	None

Auto Sales

Because automobiles are "big ticket" durable goods, monthly sales of domestically-produced autos are closely watched. However, inroads have been made by foreign competition in recent years, so the series is more indicative of the health of the domestic auto industry than of overall future economic activity.

What Does the Data Look Like?

Basically, two kinds of data are available. The first is the dollar volume of sales as reported by the Commerce Department. Sales are part of the GNP statistics discussed earlier and, like GNP, three releases are scheduled for sales in any given month: an *advance* release issued on the ninth working day of the month, a *preliminary* estimate near the end of the month, and a *final* revised release available at the close of the second month.

The second type of data, and that which receives the most attention, is in millions of units sold annually.

Unit Automotive Sales

The BEA in the Department of Commerce compiles a ***domestic car sales, seasonally adjusted annual rate*** series based on three monthly 10-day samples. The first sample period covers days 1-10 and is called the early month sample. The mid-month sample covers days 11-20 and the late-month sample covers days 21-30. The unit sales of American-made cars are adjusted for seasonal factors and converted to an annual rate to indicate the number of automobiles that would be sold if production continued at the 10-day sample rate for a twelve-month period. This information is usually available at the end of the week following the sample period.

The series, shown in Figure 4-3 below, indicates wide fluctuations from one month to the next. For example, unit auto sales in November 1988 were 7.244 million after seasonal adjustments. This increased to 8.39 million in December 1988 -- for a *monthly* change of 15.8 percent -- and then dropped 16.1 percent in January to a 7.04 million unit annual rate. High interest rates, unseasonable weather, and incentive programs by manufacturers all contribute to the monthly variations, even though the data are seasonally adjusted.

Figure 4-3
U.S. Auto Sales, Seasonally Adjusted Annual Rates

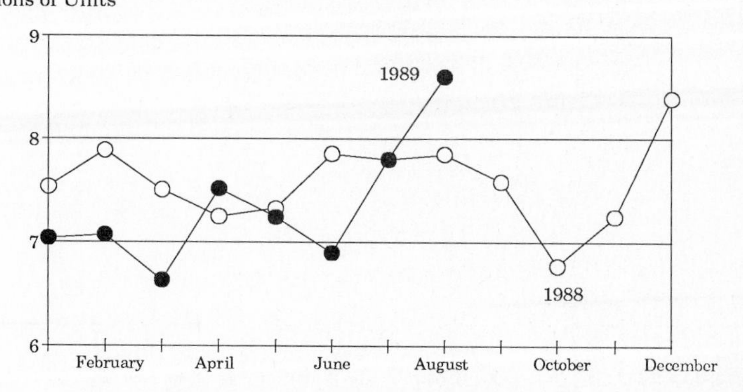

To smooth out the monthly fluctuations, the industry likes to compare sales in the most recent period to sales in the same period one year earlier. As a result, July 1989 sales were reported as essentially flat since they were compared to sales in July 1988 rather than June 1989.

Because of the small number of domestic automotive manufacturers, it is also possible to obtain unit sales directly from companies, as well as from sources like Ward's Automotive Report or the Motor Vehicle Manufacturers' Association. These sources are frequently used by financial publications to obtain extremely detailed breakdowns. For instance, the monthly summary published by *The Wall Street Journal* lists sales of approximately 25 individual domestic and foreign manufacturers, including Alfa Romeo, Range Rover, and Daihatsu. Sales by each manufacturer is divided into domestic and foreign produced units, including light trucks.

Despite the amazing degree of detail available on automotive production, even the BEA does not publish historical data, although it can be obtained on special request.

In Brief

Statistic	*Domestic Car Sales, Seasonally Adjusted Annual Rate*
Compiled by	Bureau of Economic Analysis
Frequency	Every 10 days
Release date	Week following close of 10-day period
Published data	Historical data not published by BEA, but is available on request.
Hotline update	None

Consumer Expectations

Since the consumer sector makes up such a large portion of the overall economy, it is reasonable to assume that consumer expectations about the future would have a bearing on current decisions to spend or save. This assumption is often called upon to predict future economic activity.

The Consumer Confidence Survey

The most comprehensive series, the ***consumer confidence survey***, is compiled by The Conference Board and released monthly.[3] The actual survey of consumers takes place during the first two weeks of every month and 5,000 households are covered. Data are then compiled and released during the first week of the following month.

The consumer confidence index has a base of 1985 = 100 and covers a number of categories. The major ones include appraisals of the current business situation; expectations of business conditions, employment, and income for the next six months; plans to buy automobiles, homes, and major appliances in the next six months; and questions on vacation plans. This index is available on a regional basis and is also broken down by age of household head and household income.

Overall, the series works fairly well as a leading indicator. Although no figure is shown, the series tends to peak before the

---

[3] See the *Consumer Confidence Survey*, a monthly report from the Consumer Research Center, The Conference Board, 845 Third Ave, New York, New York, 10022

economy peaks and then turn up before the economy turns up. It can be somewhat volatile with monthly changes sometimes in excess of 10 percent, but it is widely watched by the business community as an indicator of future consumer spending.

Consumer Sentiment

The Institute for Social Research at the University of Michigan compiles another survey of consumers called the ***index of consumer sentiment***. The index is based on a random monthly sample of 500 selected from all states except Alaska and Hawaii. The sample is closed, which means that only the individuals initially selected for the sample are contacted for the survey. Since the sample is random, a new group of consumers appears in the sample every month.[4] The series is shown in Figure 4-4 below:

Figure 4-4
Index of Consumer Sentiment

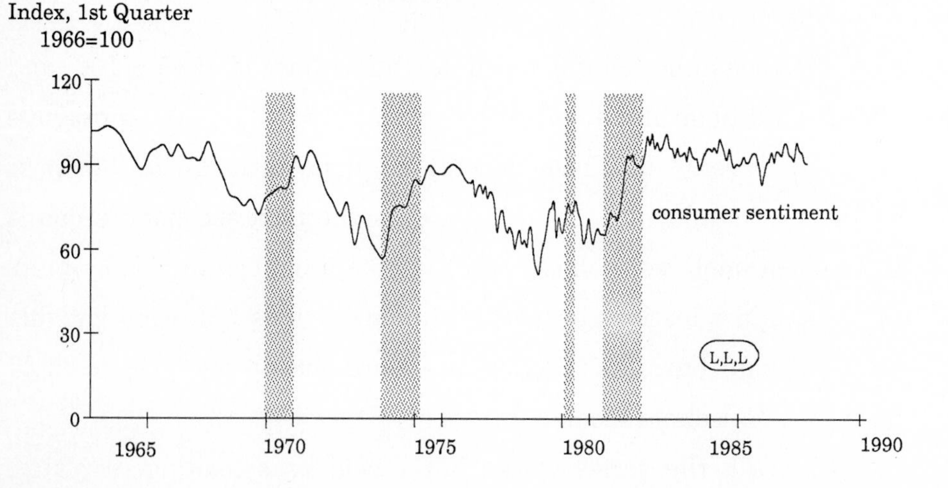

[4] Although some respondents may be contacted again later on for specialized tracking purposes.

The survey covers five major categories which are reported as separate indices: personal finance, current and expected; business conditions, current and expected; and buying conditions. The results of the survey are compiled and made available for release no later than the first week of the following month.[5]

As can be seen in the figure above, the index seems to behave fairly well as an indicator of future economic activity. Specifically, the index begins to turn down before the economy turns down and usually turns up just as or before the economy turns up.

In fact, one of the subcomponents of the consumer sentiment series, the ***index of consumer expectations***, performs so well as an indicator of future economic activity that it is included as one of the individual components in the composite *index of eleven leading indicators* put out by the U.S. Department of Commerce.

In Brief

Statistic	*Consumer Confidence* (The Conference Board) *Index of Consumer Sentiment* (Institute for Social Research, Univ of Michigan
Frequency	Monthly (both)
Release date	First week of following month (both)
Published data	*Consumer Confidence Survey*, a monthly Conference Board report *Business Conditions Digest*, for consumer sentiment data
Hotline update	(202)898-2450 for updates leading index component series as they become available

[5] The monthly reports are available on a subscription basis. For further information contact Surveys of Consumers, 426 Thompson, 3254 ISR, University of Michigan, Ann Arbor, Michigan, 48106.

Durable Goods Orders

Durable goods constitute such an important part of the overall economy, approximately 21.6 percent of total GNP in 1988, that separate statistics are often kept. We must be careful to distinguish, however, between those durables which are intended for the consumer sector and those intended for use by the business sector.

The series called ***manufacturers' new orders, durable goods industries*** is a measure of the durables goods intended for the business sector.[6] This statistic, representing less than 3 percent of total GNP, is compiled monthly from survey data and is released about three weeks after the end of the month.

How Do Durable Goods *Orders* Differ From *Production*?

There are several important differences. First, there is the difference in coverage mentioned above, with the series on durable goods orders representing a much smaller portion of GNP. Second, the Federal Reserve System collects data on the production of all durables, whereas the Bureau of Economic Analysis and the Bureau of the Census (both part of the U.S. Department of Commerce) collect data on durable goods orders.

Third, data on durable goods orders are reported in billions of dollars, rather than in the form of an index. The series is available both in terms of current dollars (using prices prevailing at the time

[6] This series is sometimes confused with another index, ***manufacturers' new orders, consumer goods and materials industries***, which is one of the 11 components of the ***index of leading indicators***.

the statistic was compiled) and in constant 1982 dollars (in terms of the prices prevailing in 1982). For the most part, the series in constant dollars, shown in Figure 4-5 below, is the more useful of the two because the distortions of inflation have been removed.

Figure 4-5
Manufacturers' New Orders, Durable Goods

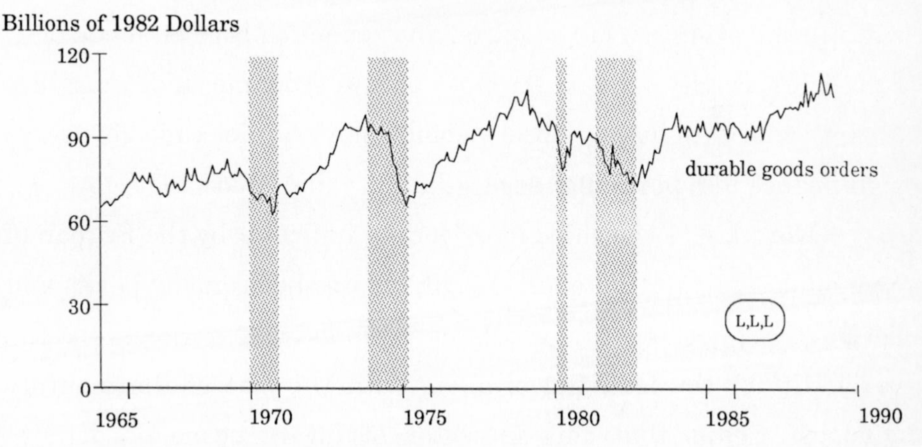

Just How Useful Is the Series?

Overall, the series gives an uneven performance as a leading indicator because it is fairly volatile in the short run. During the 24 months in 1987-88, a period of steady economic growth, the series on durable goods orders changed direction 13 times. In addition, some of the monthly changes were quite dramatic.

In May 1988, for example, the level of durable goods orders amounted to $101.74 billion (in 1982 dollars). The very next month it increased to $110.23 billion, a change of 8.3 percent in one month! In July it dropped back down to $101.67 billion, a 7.76 percent decline, and then promptly increased 5.49 percent the month after that!

Whenever a statistical series exhibits this much volatility, it is difficult to infer much from the monthly changes. It is more useful when looked at over a longer period of time, or it may be better to use some kind of moving average to smooth out the short-term changes.

Unfortunately, large changes in any statistical series can capture the attention of the press, and too much is often made of it. This is especially true when most of the economic indicators are giving mixed signals, since people may be looking for more significance in a particular series than is warranted.

Overall, it is classified as a leading indicator by the Bureau of Economic Analysis. It tends to peak before the economy peaks and bottoms out before the economy bottoms out. However, the variability of the lead times, along with the size of the monthly changes, means that this indicator of future economic activity should be used with caution.

In Brief

Statistic	*Manufacturers' New Orders Durable Goods*
Compiled by	U.S. Department of Commerce
Frequency	Monthly
Release date	Third week following the end of month
Published data	*Business Conditions Digest* *Survey of Current Business*
Hotline update	None

New Plant and Equipment Expenditures

The business sector, the third largest component of the economy (after the consumer and government sectors), consumes approximately 18 percent of total GNP. The ***expenditures for new plant and equipment*** series compiled by the Bureau of Economic Analysis tracks slightly more than half of all expenditures by business, or approximately 10 percent of total GNP expenditures.

Why are plant and equipment expenditures by business so important?

The Search for Stable Relationships

It turns out that total spending by the business sector is the most *unstable* component of the total economy. This is fairly easy to observe given the wealth of statistics available to us today, but it wasn't always that way.

In fact, when Keynes wrote his magnificent General Theory during the great depression of the 1930s, there were no GNP statistics to consult.[7] Instead, he offered a conceptual framework that broke the economy down into sectors, and then proceeded to describe, in considerable detail, the spending behavior of each. Among other things, he argued that spending by the consumer sector was relatively stable and that the spending by the business sector was unstable.

---

[7] John Maynard Keynes, The General Theory of Employment, Interest and Money, 1936.

This was an important part of his theory, because if it could be shown that the greater part of total economic activity (consumer spending) behaved in a stable and predictable manner, the instability of the total economy could be traced to a smaller component, specifically spending by the business sector.

His description of how spending takes place was so detailed that other academicians started collecting data to test his theories. In the end, the data largely confirmed the propositions put forth in the General Theory. Before long the data grew into the GNP accounts that we use today.

The National Income and Product Accounts (NIPA)

In 1988, $4,864.3 billion of final goods and services were produced in the United States. The consumption of this output by the consumer, business, and government sectors, along with $94.6 billion of imports, is shown in Table 4-2.

Table 4-2
Consumption of 1988 GNP by Sector, Billions of Current Dollars

Gross National Product					$4,864.3
Personal Consumption Expenditures[1]				3,227.5	
Gross Private Domestic Investment[2]				***766.5***	
Fixed Investment			718.1		
Nonresidential		488.4			
Structures	142.8				
Producers' durable equipment	345.6				
Residential		229.7			
Change in business inventories			48.4		
Government Purchases of Goods and Services[3]				964.9	
Net Exports of Goods and Services[4]				-94.6	

[1] Consumer sector
[2] Business sector
[3] Government sector
[4] Foreign sector

Note that total spending by the business sector amounted to $766.5 billion in 1988. The new plant and equipment expenditures series compiled by the BEA parallels the spending in the fixed investment category of total business spending but is not exactly equal to it.

Although this may appear to be a small difference, we want to distinguish between the new plant and equipment expenditure series and some of the business sector spending categories (nonresidential construction, producers' durable equipment, total fixed investment) that are widely reported in the in press.[8]

The Historical Record

The new plant and equipment expenditure series, plotted in Figure 4-6 below, gives us a feel for the stability (or lack thereof) of spending by the business sector:

Figure 4-6
New Plant and Equipment Expenditures

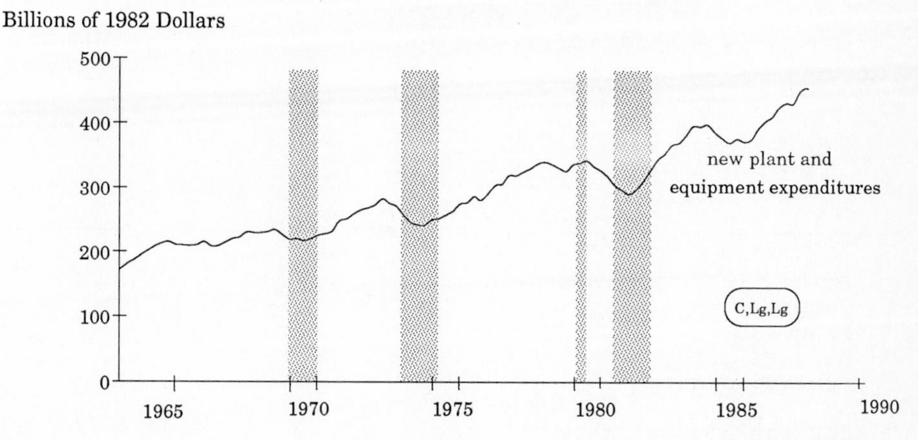

8 For example, plant and equipment expenditures are often confused with fixed investment expenditures.

The instability of business spending is especially evident when the figure above is compared to consumer spending in Figure 4-1 earlier. For example, new plant and equipment expenditures in constant dollars *dropped* a total of 13.5 percent during the 1981-1982 recession. During the same period, spending by the consumer sector (also measured in constant dollars) actually *increased* by 2.3 percent!

We have seen other statistics that move 10 to 15 percent in a month, but they represent only a small part of the total economy. Since plant and equipment expenditures represent a significant portion of the overall spending, even a small decline will have an impact on GNP.[9]

Finally, expenditures for new plant and equipment tend to move with the overall economy when the economy peaks. However, the series also lags the economic recovery which makes it a lagging indicator overall.

In Brief

Statistic	*Expenditures for New Plant and Equipment*
Compiled by	Bureau of Economic Analysis
Frequency	Quarterly
Release date	End of month with GNP revisions
Published data	*Business Conditions Digest* *Survey of Current Business*
Hotline update	None

[9] As students of economics well know, even small changes in investment spending have a way of making themselves larger through the workings of the multiplier and accelerator principles.

Corporate Profits

The Bureau of Economic Analysis in the Department of Commerce compiles several series on corporate profits. The most important is ***net profits after tax, all manufacturing corporations.***[10] All series on corporate profits are available only on a quarterly basis.

The Historical Record

Quarterly corporate profits on an inflation adjusted basis are shown in Figure 4-7 below.

Figure 4-7
Corporate Profits After Tax, Constant Dollar Basis

Billions of 1982 Dollars

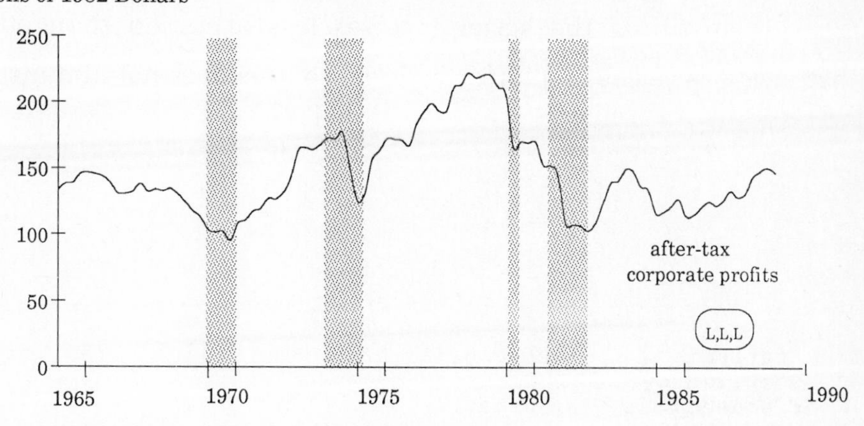

---

[10] Another series, ***corporate profits with inventory valuation and capital consumption adjustments,*** measures income *before* taxes when income is broadly defined as receipts less expenses. For a more detailed discussion of this series, see *Business Statistics 1986*, Methodological Notes for Appendix II.

Corporate Profits As a Leading Indicator?

We often think of the net corporate profits series as being an indicator of the general financial health of the corporate sector. Indeed, this is exactly what the series is intended to measure.

At the same time, it turns out that the series tends to be a leading indicator of future economic activity. In fact, this is the case even when the series is measured in terms of current (inflation biased) dollars. With the single exception of the 1973-1974 recession, corporate profits turned down well in advance of the general decline in economic activity. The series also recovered slightly before the recession ended and the economy improved.

Because of these patterns, the Bureau of Economic Analysis has classified the net corporate profits series as an overall leading indicator of future economic activity. The extent of the warning given by changes in the direction of the series may vary some, but it does give us some advance warning of future economic trends.

If anything, the series receives less attention than others because it is released quarterly. Even so, this does not diminish its usefulness.

In Brief

Statistic	*Net Profits After Tax, all Manufacturing*
Compiled by	Bureau of Economic Analysis
Frequency	Quarterly
Release date	End of month (monthly revisions are reported along with GNP revisions)
Published data	*Survey of Current Business* *Business Conditions Digest*
Hotline update	(202)898-2451 for a 3-5 minute tape when updates of GNP are available

Chapter 5
PRICES, MONEY, AND INTEREST RATES

The Consumer Price Index

The consumer price index is one of the most comprehensive statistical measures compiled by the Bureau of Labor Statistics. In fact, the BLS actually computes two measures. The first is the **CPI for all urban consumers** (**CPI-U**), which covers about 80 percent of the total population. The second, which overlaps the first, is the **CPI for urban wage earners and clerical workers** (**CPI-W**) and covers about 32 percent of the population.

When consumer prices are reported, the reference is to the CPI-U because of its broader coverage. The CPI-U is also used to calculate Social Security adjustments and is the basis for most other inflation adjustments as well.

Constructing the Sample

The index is based on a hypothetical "market basket" of goods and services that consumers buy for day-to-day living. Price changes are determined by repricing the same market basket over and over again at regular (usually monthly) intervals and comparing the total cost of the most recent market basket with the cost of the sample basket in some base period.

The selection of the types of items (not the brand names) consumers purchased most for the sample was based on surveys of consumers in 1982-1984. From this, the BLS constructed a market basket containing approximately 364 items to include in the monthly analysis.

The entries in Table 5-1 illustrate the process. First, seven major product groups (PGs, such as food and beverages, housing, and transportation) were identified. Next, the product groups were divided into 69 expenditure classes (ECs). The ECs were then divided into 207 different "strata," or types of items, and finally, 364 "entry level items" (ELIs) were selected. The latter represent the individual items in the survey whose prices will be tallied and then compared to their prices in a base period.

Table 5-1
Entry Level Items In the CPI

PG#1: Food and Beverages
    EC#1: Cereals and Cereal Products
        Strata #1: Flour and prepared flour mixes
            ELI#1: Flour
            ELI#2: Prepared flour mixes
        Strata #2: Cereal
            ELI#3: Cereal
        Strata #3: Rice, pasta, and cornmeal
            ELI#4: Rice
            ELI#5: Macaroni, similar products, and cornmeal
    EC#2: Bakery Products
PG#2: Housing
. . .
PG#6: Entertainment
PG#7: Other Goods and Services

As you can see in the table, five items (starting with flour and ending with macaroni, similar products, and cornmeal) represent the cereals and cereal products expenditure class. Each of the remaining expenditure classes are stratified, and items are selected for each strata, until 364 entry level items are available for the sample.

Using cereal for our example, let's examine how BLS determines where and how to price it. First, BLS identifies 95 geographically distributed sampling areas containing approximately 25,000 outlets to be visited every month. At each outlet a BLS field survey representative selects a particular brand of cereal based on probability techniques. For example, each brand in a given store might be assigned a weight based on the relative amount of shelf space it occupied.[1] A random number table is then used to select one of the brands for inclusion in the sample. Since this process also goes on at other outlets, different name brands are chosen so that all brands appear in the total sample in some fashion. Once the individual prices are collected from the outlets, the average price of a box of cereal is obtained.

In all, prices are collected on 95,000 items every month. For other categories, such as housing, BLS collects monthly prices from approximately 20,000 owner and 40,000 rental units. The amount of effort expended every month to compile a simple index of consumer prices is staggering!

When average prices are determined for each item in the market basket, they are added up and then expressed as a percent of their 1982-1984 total. When the CPI reached 123.8 in May 1989, it means that the total market basket now amounts to 123.8 percent of its base period cost, or that a representative item costing $1 in the base period now costs almost $1.24.

---

[1] We say "might" because other probability techniques are also used.

The Historical Record

The purpose of the CPI is to keep track of prices over time. It bears little relationship to the trends in overall economic activity as evident in Figure 5-1 below.

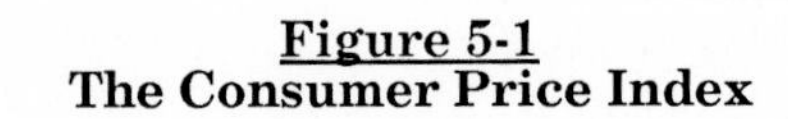
Figure 5-1
The Consumer Price Index

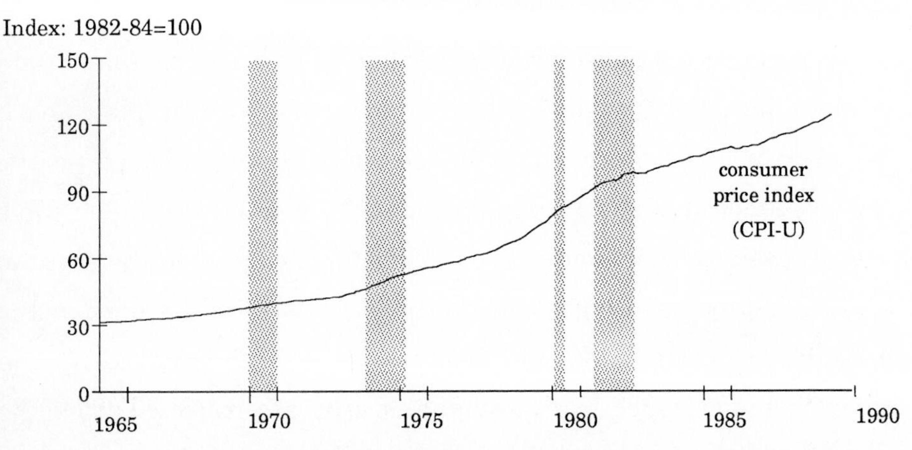

The series above reports the *level* of prices as measured by the CPI. In order to find the rate of inflation, we need to compute the change in the CPI.

One method used by the Bureau of Labor Statistics is to compute the percentage change in the CPI for the most recent month, adjust the change for seasonal variations, and then convert it to an annualized basis.[2] Since annualized estimates based on one-month changes in the CPI results in relatively wide swings in the inflation rate, it is sometimes preferable to compute the change in the CPI over longer periods. The rate of inflation as measured using changes in the CPI over 6-month spans is shown in Figure 5-2 below:

---

[2] Unfortunately, we do not know the magnitude of the seasonal adjustments, so any estimates we might make of annualized inflation based on a one-month change in the CPI may not agree with the Bureau's estimates.

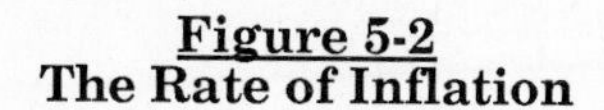

Figure 5-2
The Rate of Inflation

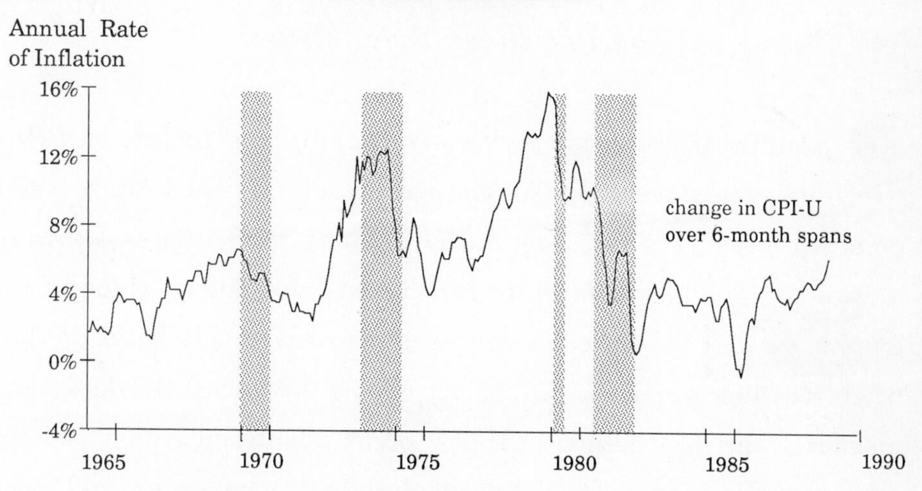

As long as the CPI is rising, then the inflation rate will be positive. Recessions usually take some of the steam out of price increases, but recent experience indicates that some degree of inflation is almost always present in the economy.

In Brief

Statistic	*Consumer Price Index (CPI)*
Compiled by	Bureau of Labor Statistics
Frequency	Monthly
Release date	Mid-month of following month
Published data	*Business Conditions Digest*
Hotline update	(202)523-9658 for a 4-minute update on consumer prices, producer prices and the unemployment rate. Or, (202)523-1239 for CPI only

The Producer Price Index

Another price series is the ***producer price index***, or ***PPI***, which measures average price changes in selling prices received by domestic producers for their output. Until 1978, the series was known as the ***wholesale price index***, but the title was changed to emphasize that the series measures only price changes between the producer and the *first* purchaser of the product. It does not measure price changes that occur between any other intermediaries, or even between the final wholesaler and the retailer who buys the product for resale to the public.

The Historical Record

Figure 5-3 below shows the level of the PPI since 1965. The CPI (or CPI-U to be exact) is also shown for comparison purposes:

Figure 5-3
Producer Prices and The Consumer Price Index

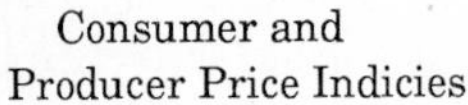

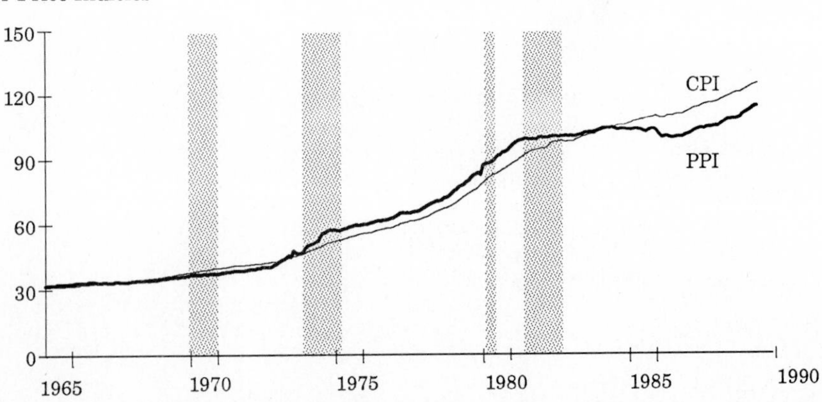

Like the CPI, the PPI is broadly based. It includes price changes in approximately 500 industries and incorporates data contained in over 3,000 separate commodity price indices.

Historically, most of the interest in producer prices has focused on their eventual impact on consumer prices. If prices go up at the factory, it stands to reason that consumers will pay more later on. Figure 5-3 above shows that there is a fairly close relationship between the two measures, although the PPI has fallen behind in recent years.

The difference is largely due to the coverage by each series. For one thing, the PPI only measures price changes when the product is first sold by the producer. If a number of intermediaries are involved, the percentage price increase to the consumer could be higher than the initial increase at the factory. For another, the PPI covers *goods*, while *services* are largely ignored. Finally, the PPI does not cover imported items which make up a substantial part of consumer purchases.

Increases in the PPI frequently lead to increases in the CPI. However, it is possible to have increases in the CPI without corresponding increases in the PPI because of the way services and imported goods are treated.

In Brief

Statistic	*Producer Price Index (PPI)*
Compiled by	Bureau of Labor Statistics
Frequency	Monthly
Release date	Mid-Month of following month
Published data	*Business Conditions Digest*
Hotline update	(202)523-9658 for a 4-minute update on consumer prices, producer prices and the unemployment rate Or, (202)523-1765 for PPI only

Money Supply

Economists define money as anything which serves as a unit of account, a medium of exchange, and a store of value. However, the exact definition of money is complicated by the fact that it takes so many different forms, ranging from coins to eurodollar deposits.[3]

Definitions of the Money

The Fed employs several definitions of money, two of which correspond to the functions of money described above.[4] One is called ***M1*** and is the transactional component of the money supply, or the part most closely identified with money's role a medium of exchange. As can be seen in Table 5-2, this definition of the money supply includes coins, paper currency, traveler's checks, demand deposits, NOW accounts, credit union share drafts, and other checkable deposits.

If we want to consider money's role as a store of value as well as a medium of exchange, the definition is expanded to include other, and sometimes lesser-known, forms of holding money. These include money market deposit accounts, saving deposits, time deposits, and Eurodollars, as well as money market funds held by institutions, money market brokers and dealers. This broader-based definition of money includes 14 separate components and is known as ***M2***. The individual components of M1 and M2, as listed in the weekly Fed release H.6, are presented in Table 5-2 below.

---

[3] Eurodollar deposits are dollar-denominated deposits in banks located in foreign countries.
[4] A total of four definitions -- M1, M2, M3, and L -- are currently used by the Fed.

Table 5-2
Components of the Money Supply, Billions of Current Dollars*

1.	Coins and paper currency	$216.6	
2.	Traveler's checks	7.1	
3.	Demand deposits	273.4	
4.	Other checkable deposits (NOW accts, share drafts)	270.2	
	M1		**$767.3**
5.	Overnight repurchase agreements	$57.9	
6.	Overnight Eurodollars	14.7	
7.	General purpose and broker/dealer money market funds	259.9	
8.	Money market deposit accounts	457.0	
9.	Savings deposits	407.4	
10.	Small denomination time deposits	1,099.2	
11.	Large denomination time deposits	569.7	
12.	Institution-only money market funds	91.6	
13.	Term repurchase agreements	127.6	
14.	Term Eurodollars	101.4	
	M2 = (M1 plus lines 5-14)		**$3,953.7**

* as of May 1989

The Historical Record

Since the money supply is managed by the Federal Reserve System, we would expect that some variation in the money stock is possible over time. Money (like any other commodity) can also be measured in terms of current or real dollar amounts, although the latter is preferable if we want to compensate for the distortions of inflation. Figure 5-4 below shows the levels of M1 and M2 from 1965 to the present. The figure also reveals that both definitions of the money stock tend to act as leading indicators, although there is more variation in M2 than in M1.

Figure 5-4
M1 and M2 in Constant Dollars, 1965-present

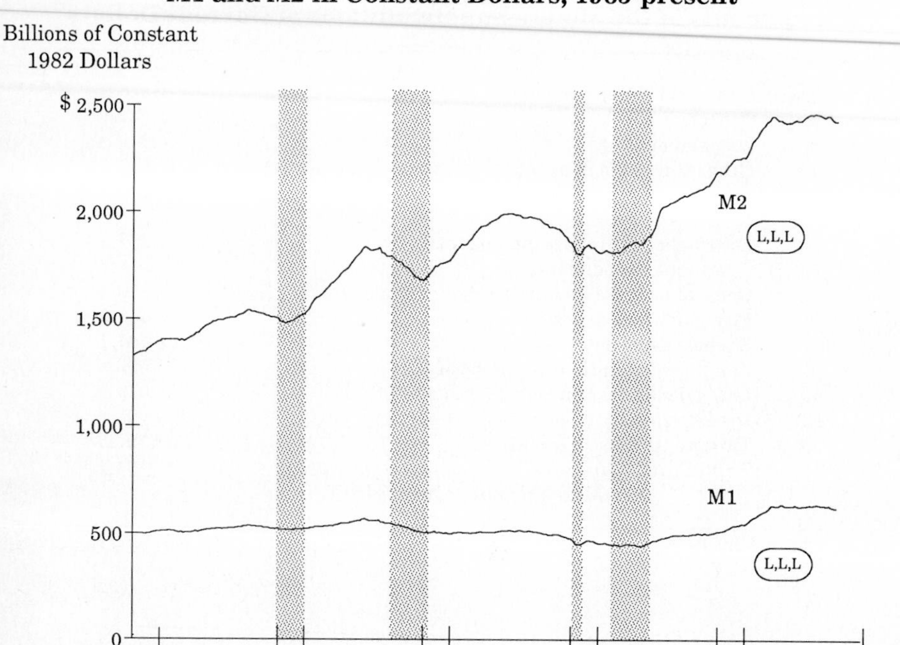

The wider fluctuations in M2 is due to the monetary policy actions of the Fed. Whether intentionally or not, M2 behaves in a reliable and predictable pattern, so much so that it has been classified as a leading indicator for both recessions and recoveries. In fact, it is so reliable that it is included as one of the component series in the composite *index of eleven leading indicators.*

In Brief

Statistic	*M1, M2*
Compiled by	The Fed Board of Governors
Frequency	Weekly
Release date	4:30pm Thursdays for previous week
Published data	*Fed Statistical Release H.6 (508)* *Federal Reserve Bulletin*
Hotline update	None

The Prime Rate

Historically, the ***prime rate*** was the rate banks charged its best customers. Because of this, it received wide publicity as the lowest rate available from banks. The prime rate is not quite the same as the rate actually paid, but it is still widely watched.

If You Get the Prime Rate, Do You Actually Pay It?

That depends. Suppose a business borrows $100,000 at a 10 percent prime rate. However, the company may not get the use of all of the funds because the bank may require a *compensating balance*, or a deposit (usually interest free) in the amount of $5,000. On a simple interest basis, the company is really paying $10,000 to get the use of $95,000, for a 10.53 percent simple rate.

Another bank may have an identical prime, but a different compensating balance requirement in the amount of $10,000 per $100,000 borrowed. A borrower at this bank would still pay 10 percent on the $100,000 for an interest cost of $10,000 but only have access to $90,000, for an 11.11 percent simple rate.

The Historical Record

Figure 5-5 on the next page shows that the prime rate appears to adjust in steps, or stages. That is, it will stay at one level for awhile and then adjust to a new one. There are two reasons for this. First, banks are more inclined to change the compensating balance requirement rather than the prime, especially when interest rates are rising. Second, the official prime rate statistics compiled by the Fed represent the prevailing level, rather than averages of the existing rates charged by banks.

Figure 5-5
The Average Prime Rate Charged by Banks

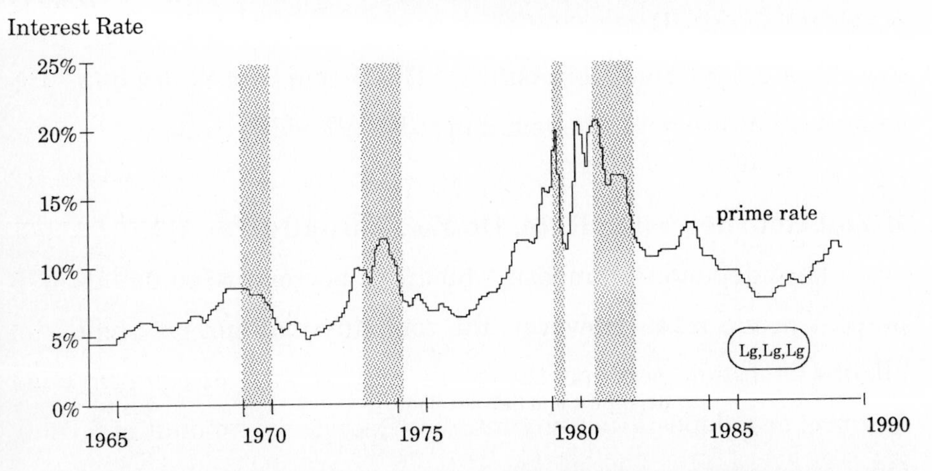

The Fed determines the predominant prime rate by surveying the 29 major banks listed in Table 5-3. Once the predominant prime is established, the Fed waits for 15 of the 29 banks to adopt a new rate before the prime is recomputed. Occasionally, a bank not on the list may change its rate, and the action may be widely reported in the press, but it will have no effect on the official predominant prime rate statistics compiled by the Fed.

Because banks can increase effective interest rates by changing the compensating balance rather than the prime, the prime is a lagging indicator for both recessions and recoveries. Changes in the prime rate usually make headlines, but the changes usually only reflect other interest rate changes that have already taken place.

Table 5-3
Banks Included in Determination of Predominant Prime Rate

District 1	The First National Bank of Boston
District 2	Bankers Trust Company
	The Chase Manhattan Bank, N.A.
	Chemical Bank
	Citibank, N.A.
	Irving Trust Company
	Manufacturers Hanover Trust Company
	Marine Midland Bank, N.A.
	Morgan Guaranty Trust Company of N.Y.
District 3	First Pennsylvania Bank, N.A.
	Mellon Bank (East), N.A.
	Philadelphia National Bank
District 4	Ameritrust Company, N.A.
	Mellon Bank, N.A.
	Pittsburgh National Bank
District 7	Continental Illinois National Bank & Trust Company of Chicago
	Comerica Bank-Detroit
	The First National Bank of Chicago
	Harris Trust and Savings Bank
	Manufacturers National Bank of Detroit
	The Northern Trust Company
District 12	Bank of America
	Bank of California, N.A.
	Seattle-First National Bank
	Security Pacific National Bank
	Union Bank
	First Interstate Bank of California
	Wells Fargo Bank, N.A.

Source: The Federal Reserve System

In Brief

Statistic	*Prime Rate*
Compiled by	Fed Board of Governors
Frequency	Weekly
Release date	Monday of every week for previous week
Published data	*Fed Reserve Bulletin* and *Selected Interest Rates,* Fed release H.15(519) *Business Conditions Digest*
Hotline update	No direct hotline since the Fed is not authorized to give out interest rates over the phone. However, other data is available on (202)452-6459

The Discount Rate

In its role as a central bank, the Federal Reserve System is required to lend funds to other financial institutions. The **discount rate** is the interest rate the Fed charges on these borrowed funds. Unlike other interest rates, the discount rate is a tool of monetary policy used by the Fed to control the money supply. As such, the discount rate affects the general level of credit, and eventually employment, prices, and overall economic activity economy.

Early Development

When the Fed was first organized in 1913, the discount rate was intended to be the primary tool of monetary policy used to influence interest rates. In the 1920s, however, the Fed discovered that interest rates could also be affected by buying and selling government bonds, a function now managed by the Federal Open Market Committee (FOMC).

It may seem redundant to have an independently determined discount rate coexist with FOMC activities, but this arrangement has two advantages for the Fed. First, the discount rate is set in conjunction with the regional Fed banks, fostering an appearance of participation in the monetary policy decision-making process. Second, it generates an "announcement effect" which serves as a source of policy information for Fed-watchers.[5]

[5] A recent article in *Economic Commentary* by the Federal Reserve Bank of Cleveland explains how the discount rate is set:

The Historical Record

Because the discount rate is discretionary, it changes only infrequently as shown in Figure 5-6 below:

Figure 5-6
The Discount Rate

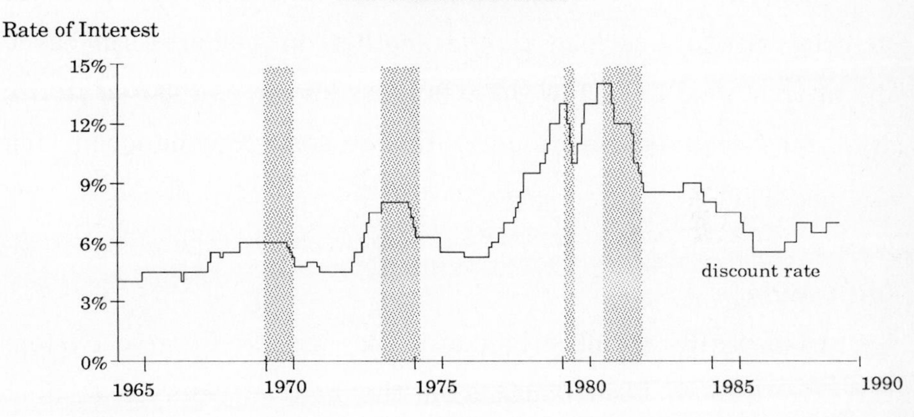

The rise in the discount rate at the end of each expansion in Figure 5-6 above reflects the Fed's concern with controlling inflation as much as anything. The discount rate is not a competitive market rate; it is a tool of monetary policy and is used to affect the overall cost of credit in the economy.

In Brief

Statistic	*The Discount Rate*
Compiled by	Fed Board of Governors
Frequency	Discretionary
Release date	None
Published data	*Federal Reserve Bulletin*
Hotline update	None

"The mechanics of setting the discount rate are not complicated. The Board of Directors of each of the 12 Federal Reserve Banks is required to recommend a rate setting for its Bank to the Board of Governors of the Federal Reserve System no less frequently than every two weeks. If the Board of Governors approves the recommendation, typically it will notify any of the other 12 Banks that have not made the same recommendation so that their Board of Directors have an opportunity to act simultaneously. If the Board of Governors thinks that a change is called for when none of the 12 Banks has recommended a change, it may make informal efforts to elicit a recommendation." (July 15, 1989)

The Fed Funds Rate

Fed funds are reserve balances that banks and other financial institutions lend to one another on a short-term basis. The interest paid to borrow these funds is known as the ***Fed funds rate***. Most loans are overnight, although some may be for as long as three days.

Fed Funds

Historically, member banks of the Federal Reserve System were required to keep deposits at the Fed as reserves against savings accounts and checking deposits. If a bank had excess reserves, it would often lend the surplus funds to another member bank on an overnight or weekend basis. Since the Fed did not pay interest on the reserves, member banks had little incentive to keep more funds than they needed with the Fed. Banks that borrowed the excess reserves often did so to shore up their own reserves which they also kept at the Fed.

When the loans were made, the funds never really left the Fed -- hence the term "Fed" for "Federal Reserve" funds. All the banks needed to do to make the transaction was notify the regional Fed bank that reserve funds were to be transferred to another bank's account for a short period of time, after which the funds would be transferred back.

Over time, Fed funds took on a more generic meaning as the practice of borrowing one another's reserves expanded to financial institutions outside the Federal Reserve System.[6] Today, financial institutions tend to deal with one another through the Fed since all depository institutions have better access to the Fed.

A Leading Indicator

The recent history of the Federal funds rate is presented in Figure 5-7 below. Like most other interest rates in the economy, it has an overall classification as a lagging indicator.

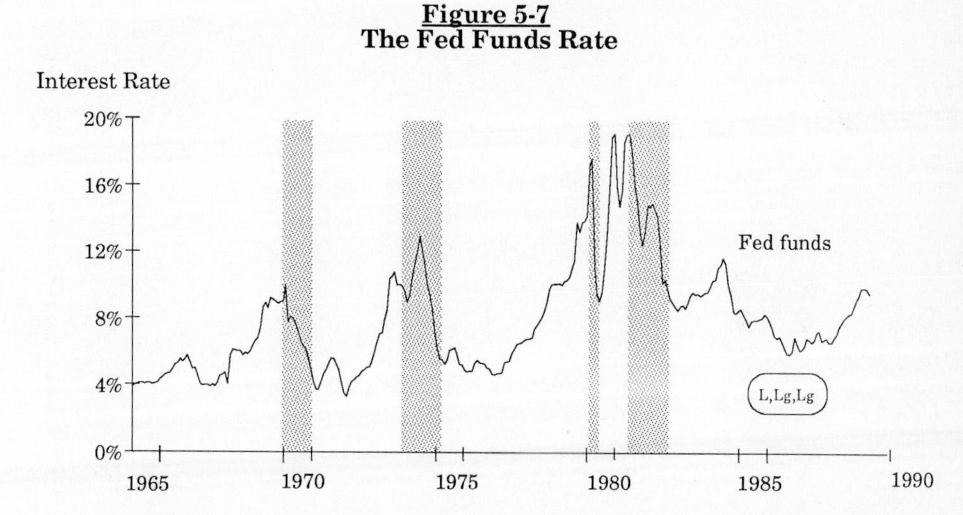

Figure 5-7
The Fed Funds Rate

Unlike other interest rates, however, it is the *only* interest rate followed by the Bureau of Economic Analysis that is classified as a leading indicator for peaks in overall economic activity. As such, it also tends to turn down before other interest rates in the economy turn down.

The reasons for this behavior are probably due to the way in which the Federal Reserve System conducts monetary policy. If the

[6] Nonmember state banks, for example, might lend reserves to one another under this system.

economy shows signs of entering a recession, the Fed may pump excess reserves into the banking system to keep the economy going. This practice increases the overall amount of reserves in the system and lowers the price that others pay to borrow them.

Because Fed funds are the only interest rate classified as a leading indicator for peaks in economic activity, they can serve both as an indicator for future changes in real GNP and as a leading indicator for movements in other interest rates.

In Brief

Statistic	*Fed Funds Rate*
Compiled by	Fed Board of Governors
Frequency	Weekly
Release date	Monday of every week for previous week
Published data	*Fed Reserve Bulletin* and *Selected Interest Rates,* Fed release H.15(519) *Business Conditions Digest*
Hotline update	None

Treasury Bill Rate

The ***Treasury bill rate*** is one of the most important interest rate in the economy. Treasury bills (t-bills) are auctioned weekly and traded daily, so the rate on t-bills reflects the most current market forces of supply and demand.

The Historical Record

The history of interest rate movements for treasury bills is shown in Figure 5-8 below. For purposes of comparison, the prime rate is plotted as well:

Figure 5-8
Treasury Bill Rates and Aggregate Economic Activity

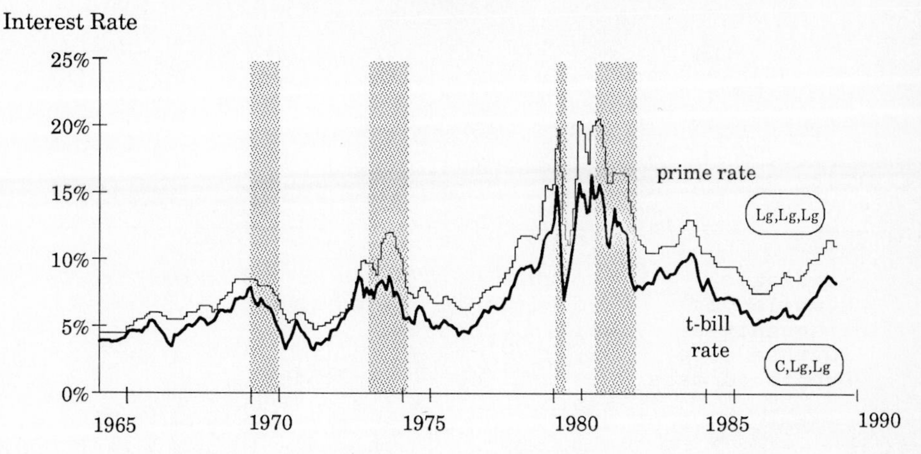

A Coincident-Lagging Indicator

Since the t-bill rate adjusts immediately to market forces, it changes earlier than the prime. The series behaves as a coincident indicator for peaks in the economy, meaning that the rate turns down when the economy turns down.

It also behaves as a lagging indicator when the economy recovers from a recession, meaning that the economy recovers before the t-bill rates recover. In all, the classification of the t-bill series, like that of almost all interest rate series, is that of lagging indicator.

Treasury bills are traded continuously during market hours so rates are available daily. Summary information is published by the Fed and most financial newspapers. Because the t-bill rate is so competitive, many adjustable rate financial securities, including some home mortgages, are tied to them.

In Brief

Statistic	*Treasury Bill Rate*
Compiled by	Fed Board of Governors
Frequency	Daily
Release date	Daily
Published data	Most financial newspapers Fed statistical release H.15 (519), released Monday for week ended previous Saturday *Business Conditions Digest* *Survey of Current Business*
Hotline update	No direct hotline since the Fed is not authorized to give out interest rates over the phone. However, other data is available on (202)452-6459

Chapter 6
FINANCIAL MARKETS

The Dow Jones Industrial Average

The ***Dow Jones Industrial Average* (DJIA)** is one of the oldest and most quoted measures of stock market performance in the United States. It is used as a proxy for the price movements of approximately 1650 stocks on the New York Stock Exchange.

The DJIA includes 30 representative firms, and the size of the index depends on the market price of each firm's stock at any given time. If the prices of the stocks in the average are rising, the DJIA goes up and the market is also presumed to be going up. If the prices of the 30 stocks are falling, the DJIA goes down, indicating that other stocks in the market are also going down.

Over time, some firms are deleted and others added to keep the representation current, but the total number of stocks is kept at 30.

Early History

In 1884, the Dow Jones Corporation began to publish the average closing price of 11 active stocks in its *Customer's Afternoon Letter*, a short publication which later evolved into *The Wall Street Journal*. By 1886, the average included 12 stocks, and by 1916 it was expanded to 20. Finally, in 1928 it was expanded to include 30 stocks, with the ones used today listed in Table 6-1 below:

Table 6-1
The 30 Stocks in the Dow Jones Industrial Average*

Allied Signal	Exxon	Philip Morris
Alcoa	General Electric	Primerica
American Express	General Motors	Procter & Gamble
American T&T	Goodyear	Sears Roebuck
Bethlehem Steel	IBM	Texaco
Boeing	International Paper	USX
Chevron	McDonald's	Union Carbide
Coca Cola	Merck	United Technologies
Du Pont	Minnesota Mining & Mfg	Westinghouse
Eastman Kodak	Navistar	Woolworth

* as of July 1989

One popular format for reporting the DJIA is shown in Figure 6-1, which represents daily movements in terms of vertical bars. Since the average moves up and down all day long, the top of the

Figure 6-1
The Dow Jones Industrial Average

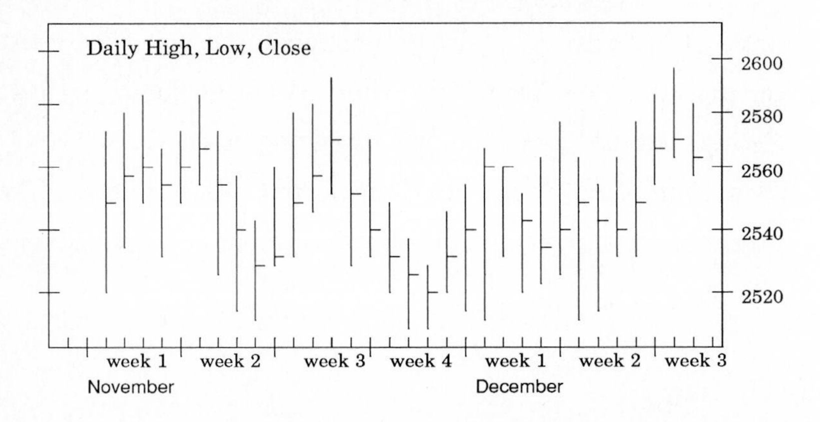

bar represents the highest value for the DJIA, and the bottom the lowest value. The little nub on the side of the bar represents the closing value for the day. Note that we cannot tell the time of day the high and low values were reached, the chart only tells us the range.

But Is It *Really* an Average?

In 1884 when it was first compiled, the DJIA really was an average. However, as some stocks began to split, it caused computational problems for the index. For example, consider a simple DJIA, with three stocks priced \$20, \$30, and \$40. The average for the group is \$30, or simply 30. Suppose the next day that nothing happens except for a two-for-one split of the \$20 stock (instead of holding one share of \$20 stock, you own two at \$10, so your wealth remains unchanged.)

If we report the DJIA at the end of the second day by dividing the prices of three shares (\$10, \$30 and \$40) by three, the DJIA drops to 23.3 from 30, even though investors are no worse off than before. We could, however, compensate for the drop in the average by adjusting the *divisor*. Instead of dividing the sum of the prices by 3, we could divide by 2.667 so that the "average" would be (\$10 + \$20 + \$40)/2.667 = 30, just as before.

Whenever a stock splits or whenever the list of stocks is revised, the divisor can be adjusted to keep the overall average from being affected. Of course, this means that the divisor is being revised almost constantly. By 1939, for example, the divisor was about 15 and by 1950 it was below 9. It was at 1.3 in 1981 and had reached .67 by mid-1989.[1]

In mid-June 1989, the computation was as follows:

$$\text{DJIA} = \frac{\text{sum of 30 prices}}{\text{divisor}} = \frac{\$1,684.11}{.670} = 2513.60$$

[1] On June 12, 1988, the divisor for the 30 industrials was changed from .680 to .670 when Boeing, one of the 30 industrial stocks, declared a 3-for-2 split of its common stock.

We can now definitely say that the Dow Jones Industrial Average really *is* an average ... in a manner of speaking.

Are 30 Stocks Enough?

Despite the small number of stocks represented in the DJIA, the companies are so large, and so many shares of stock are outstanding, that the DJIA represents about 25 percent of the total value of all stocks on the New York Stock Exchange. As a result, the movement of the DJIA coincides fairly well with a large number of stocks on the exchange.

The companies in the DJIA do not, however, represent the smaller companies on the exchange nor do they represent other firms listed on the American Stock Exchange or the over-the-counter market. The advantage of the DJIA is the ease of computation -- it is actually updated every five minutes -- and the visibility given to it by the Dow Jones Corporation, which publishes *The Wall Street Journal*.

Are There Other Things We Should Know?

There are probably two worth mentioning. First, any price-weighted average like the DJIA gives more weight to higher priced stocks than it does to lower priced ones. For example, a 10 percent increase in the price of Navistar (trading near $6 in mid-1989) only adds $.60 to the numerator in the equation above. A 10 percent increase in the price of IBM (trading near $110 at the same time) adds $11 to the numerator.

The other weakness of the DJIA is that it does not adjust for stock dividends of less than 10 percent.[2] This means that the DJIA understates long-term gains in the market. Stock prices will not tend to rise as fast if some companies declare relatively small and relatively frequent stock dividends.

Because the series is updated so frequently, and because it has such high visibility, it is a useful measure of short-term movements of stock prices on the New York Stock Exchange. When stock price movements over longer periods are of concern, however, researchers usually turn to other series which have a broader sample and are not biased by stock dividend payouts.

In Brief

Statistic	*Dow Jones Industrial Average*
Compiled by	The Dow Jones Corporation
Frequency	Available every 5 minutes during market hours
Published data	Daily in *The Wall Street Journal* and in the stock market section of any paper *Survey of Current Business*
Hotline update	(212)976-4141 for the latest market update from the D-Jones Market Report

[2] Theoretically, a stock dividend (a dividend paid in stock, rather than cash) *lowers* the price of a company's stock. If a firm declares an 8 percent stock dividend, the number of shares outstanding goes up by 8 percent and the price of the stock goes down by 8 percent -- leaving investors with no change in net wealth. As far as the DJIA is concerned, however, the average should go down since the price of the stock goes down.

Standard & Poor's 500

Another popular measure of stock price performance is the ***Standard & Poor's 500*** (**S&P 500**) composite index. Standard and Poor's Corporation published its first market index of 233 stocks in 1923. By 1957, the list had expanded to a total of 500 stocks. Today, those 500 stocks represent four major industry groupings: industrials, public utilities, transportations, and finance.[3]

How Are the Firms in the Index Selected?

The selection is based on industry groupings. The market is first divided into approximately 100 subgroups ranging from aerospace to toys. Then, representative companies are selected for each industry grouping. In some cases, the firms in the subgroup are relatively small, with modest stock issues outstanding.

Moreover, unlike the DJIA, the companies in the subgroupings do not have to be listed on the NYSE; many are listed on the American Stock Exchange and the over-the-counter market. While the companies in the S&P 500 do not necessarily include the largest companies on the New York Stock Exchange, approximately 80 percent of the total value of the NYSE stocks are represented in the index.

---

[3] Until recently, the 500 stocks consisted of 400 industrial companies, 40 public utilities, 20 transportation companies, and 40 financial institutions. When a company in one category was dropped, it was replaced by another company from the same category. This practice was dropped in 1988, so the number of companies in each category will vary somewhat over time.

How Is the Index Computed?

The S&P 500 is not an average like the DJIA, it is a *value-weighted index* reflecting the total market value of a company's stock. For each company in the sample, the total number of shares of the company's stock is multiplied by the individual price per share to get the total market value of that stock.[4] The market value for each of the remaining 499 stocks are computed in the same way and added together to get the current market value of all 500 stocks in the index.

The resulting number would be huge, of course, but when indexed to a base period (1941-1943 is currently used), the series becomes more manageable. It is slightly different from most other indices, as the base has a value of 10 rather than 100. So if the S&P 500 closes at 350, the total market value of all stocks in the index is 35 times higher (350/10) today than it was in the 1941-1943 period.

Is the S&P 500 Better than the DJIA?

Different perhaps, but not necessarily better. It is more representative, since 500 stocks are covered rather than 30. In addition, the value-weighted nature of the index means that it automatically adjusts for splits and stock dividends.[5]

In addition to its role as a proxy for stock price movements, the index also serves well as a leading indicator of future economic

---

[4] A company with 3 million shares of common stock outstanding, valued at $15/share, would have a total market value of (3,000,000)($15) = $60,000,000.

[5] Suppose that a company listed in the S&P 500 declares a 5 percent stock dividend. The number of shares would go up by 5 percent, the price of the shares would go down by a corresponding amount, leaving the total market value of the stock -- and the level of the S&P 500 -- unchanged. If that same company happened to be one of the 30 DJIA stocks, the index would fall slightly because the price of one of the stocks in the numerator would fall, *without* any compensating change in the divisor.

activity.[6] As shown in Figure 6-2 below, the S&P 500 usually peaks some months before the recession begins and then recovers before the economy does:

Figure 6-2
The Standard & Poor's 500 Composite Index

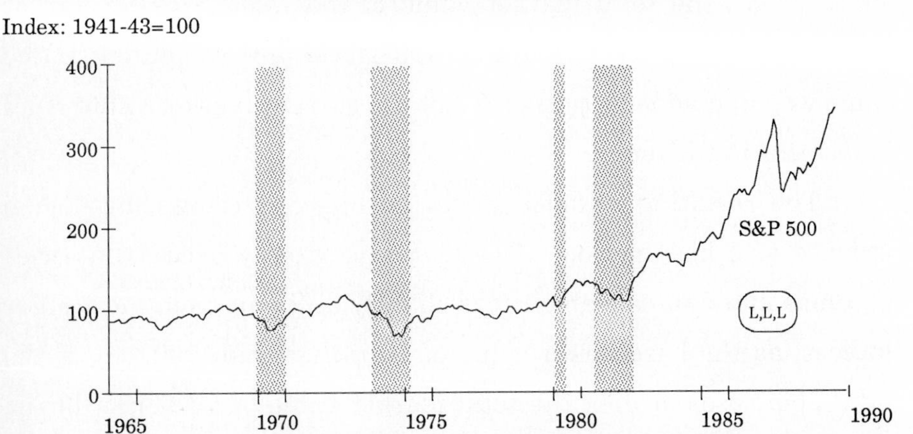

Finally, the S&P 500 is not compiled as frequently as the DJIA, and so is not quite as useful for detecting extremely short-term price movements.

In Brief

Statistic	*Standard & Poor's 500*
Compiled by	Standard & Poor's Corporation
Frequency	Hourly
Release date	Daily
Published data	Stock report in any daily paper *Business Conditions Digest* *Survey of Current Business*
Hotline update	(212)208-8706,7 or 8 for a brief tape message

[6] The S&P 500 index is one of the 11 series used in the composite ***index of leading indicators*** by the Department of Commerce.

NYSE Composite

The broadest and most comprehensive measure of stock price performance on the New York Stock Exchange is the ***NYSE composite index*** which covers *every* stock listed on the New York Stock Exchange. Subindexes are also available for industrial, utility, transportation, and financial stocks.

How Does It Differ from Other Stock Market Measures?

The biggest difference is coverage. The DJIA uses a sample of only 30 stocks from the NYSE. The S&P 500 has a larger sample but covers several major exchanges. As a result, the NYSE composite is especially attractive to investors who have all of their securities listed on that exchange.

A typical listing of the NYSE closing might appear as in Table 6-2 below:

Table 6-2
The New York Stock Exchange Composite Index*

Year			Day			Previous 12 Mos	
High	Low	Series	Close	Change	%Ch	Close	%Ch
183.18	145.94	Composite	177.90	-0.85	-.48	+24.22	+15.76
219.68	175.06	Industrials	212.91	-1.23	-.57	+27.07	+14.57
89.99	69.61	Utilities	87.30	-0.12	-.14	+14.85	+20.50
176.96	128.89	Transports	171.16	-0.45	-.26	+31.44	+15.76
156.14	126.98	Finance	151.42	-0.61	-.40	+20.32	+15.50

*Closing prices on 6/30/89

Like the S&P 500, the NYSE composite is a value-weighted index which reflects the total market value of every company listed on the exchange. When the series was first introduced on December 31, 1965, the average price of a share of stock was $50.33. By setting the base equal to 50, the composite, at least in its early years, approximated the average price of a share of stock.[7] The NYSE index is shown in Figure 6-3 below:

Figure 6-3
The NYSE Composite Index

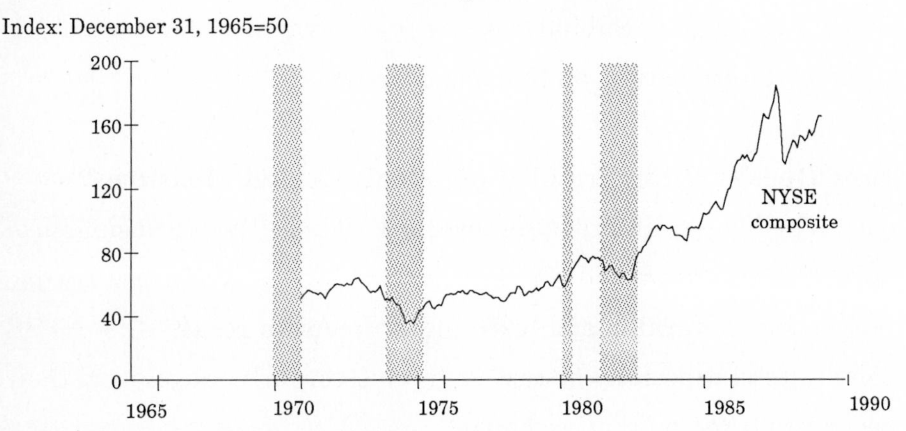

Over time, the composite index behaves like other stock price measures. It is considered a leading indicator, although it is not followed regularly by the BEA.

In Brief

Statistic	*NYSE Composite*
Compiled by	The New York Stock Exchange
Frequency	Every 30 minutes
Release date	Daily
Published data	Stock report in any daily newspaper *Survey of Current Business*
Hotline update	(212)976-4141 for the latest market update from the D-Jones Market Report

[7] However, this relationship does not hold over time, so today we focus on the percentage change in the level of the index.

Chapter 7
INTERNATIONAL TRADE AND FINANCE

The Merchandise Trade Deficit

When a country engages in international trade, it is unlikely that the value of merchandise imported will exactly offset the value of the merchandise exported. A formal set of accounts, including the ***balance on merchandise trade*** series, tracks this international flow of both durable and nondurable goods.[1]

The word "balance" in the title allows for the possibility of a surplus as well as a deficit. However, the United States has consistently imported more merchandise than it has exported since the first quarter of 1976. Because imports have exceeded imports for so long, the word *deficit* is widely used in place of *balance*. As a result, the statistic is commonly -- although improperly -- called the *merchandise trade deficit*.

The National Income and Product Accounts (Again)

The breakdown of GNP in the national income and product accounts presented in Table 7-1 below illustrates the trade balance. The structure follows the familiar approach whereby the economy

---

[1] When services are included, the series is called the ***balance on goods and services***. Historically, this has been of less interest since the large deficits appeared in the goods category.

is divided into sectors. This time, we want to focus on the foreign sector, otherwise known as "net exports of goods and services."

Table 7-1
GNP and the Merchandise Trade Balance in 1988, Billions of Current Dollars

Gross National Product				$4,864.2
Personal Consumption Expenditures			3,227.5	
Gross Private Domestic Investment			788.5	
Net Exports of Goods and Services			***-94.7***	
Exports		519.7		
Merchandise	***321.6***			
Durable Goods	201.3			
Nondurable Goods	201.3			
Services	198.2			
Imports		614.4		
Merchandise	***449.7***			
Durable Goods	295.2			
Nondurable Goods	154.5			
Services	164.7			
Government Purchases of Goods and Services			664.9	

In 1988, the total value of all exports amounted to $519.7 billion. This was offset by imports of $614.4 billion, leaving an overall deficit of $94.7 billion. Since the export and import categories are further divided into merchandise (durable and nondurable goods) and services, the trade deficit can be expressed in terms of goods only, with services being ignored.

This gives us merchandise exports of $321.6 billion and imports of $449.7 billion, leaving a balance on merchandise trade of $128.1 billion for all of 1988.

But, What About Monthly Numbers?

After all, the numbers in Table 7-1 are for the entire year, hardly a useful basis if we want to find out how we are doing at any given time.

Trade figures are collected continuously and released on both a monthly and quarterly basis. Data for merchandise exports and imports are collected by the Bureau of the Census from declarations filed with the U.S. Customs Office by shippers. Because of the nature of the data, the value of merchandise exports and imports are not released until 45 days after the month ends.

The trade figures are usually reported in terms of actual dollar amounts, without being adjusted for inflation and without being annualized. This means that the size of the deficit will be small if the report is for the month, approximately three times larger if the report is for the quarter, and approximately 12 times larger than the first figure if the report is for the year.

To illustrate, the balance on merchandise trade was a *negative* $9.762 billion in May 1988. For the second quarter (which includes May), the balance was a negative $34.606 billion; for the entire year, it was a negative $128.1 billion. Whenever trade statistics are released, we obviously need to know the coverage involved, lest we mistake a particularly large month for an unusually small quarter.

In Figure 7-1, quarterly data are used to show the balance on merchandise trade from 1965 to the present. The balance can be shown as either the difference between exports and imports, or it can be plotted separately as in the bottom of the figure.

The trade balance is dependent on two main forces: (1) our demand for foreign-made products and (2) our ability to sell domestically produced goods abroad. Both exports and imports have been affected by recessions, but the difference between the two -- the balance on merchandise trade -- is much less affected.

Figure 7-1
Exports, Imports, and the Balance on Merchandise Trade

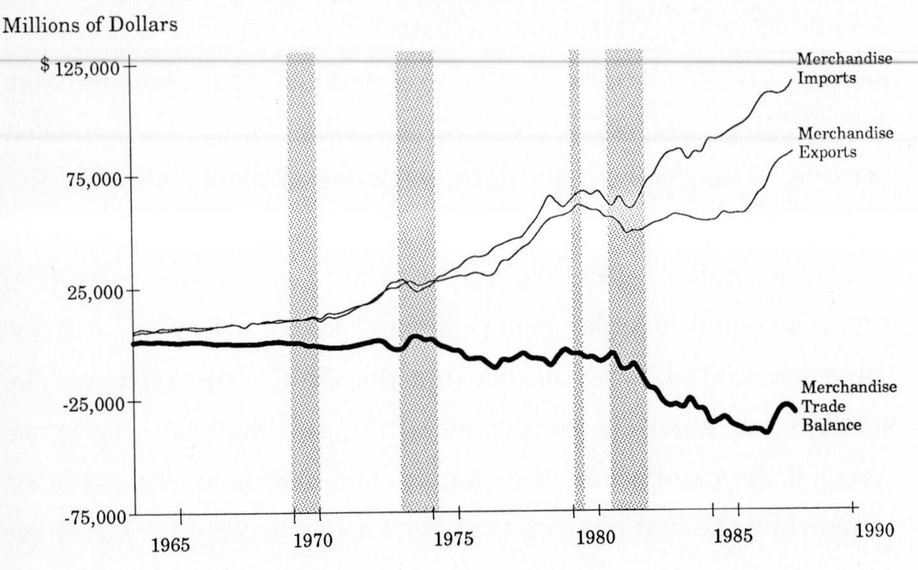

The overall balance is important because it affects employment in the export and import industries as well as the value of the U.S. dollar. Since dollars are paid to foreigners to make up for the deficit, larger deficits mean that more dollars go abroad, and more dollars circulating relative to other currencies makes the dollar worth less.

Finally, we note that the overall trade figures can be broken down by individual countries, so it is not unusual to see a balance on merchandise trade report for a single country rather than for all countries together.

In Brief

Statistic	*Balance on Merchandise Trade*
Compiled by	Bureau of the Census
Frequency	monthly, quarterly
Release date	45 days after close of reporting month
Published data	*Survey of Current Business* *Business Conditions Digest* *Federal Reserve Bulletin*
Hotline update	None

Foreign Exchange

The ***foreign exchange rate*** is defined as the rate at which one country's currency is exchanged for another. Since there are well over 200 currencies in the world today, there are a quite number of ways in which a single exchange rate can be reported.

Currency per U.S. Dollar

One popular way to express an exchange rate is in terms of foreign currency units purchased with *one* U.S. dollar. For example, if 1.8917 German marks could be purchased with one U.S. dollar, then the exchange rate for the mark would be 1.8917 to 1. Likewise, an exchange rate of 139.08 to 1 for the Japanese yen means that 139.08 yen could be purchased with one U.S. dollar. In each case, the rate is expressed in terms of the number of foreign currency units that could be purchased with one U.S. dollar.

U.S. Dollar Equivalents

A second way to express a foreign exchange rate is in terms of U.S. dollar equivalents. This time we state the dollar value of *one* foreign currency unit.

If we can purchase 1.8917 German marks with one dollar, then the value of one mark would be $.5286 U.S. (the reciprocal of 1.8917). Likewise, the U.S. dollar equivalent value of one Japanese yen is 1/139.08, or $.0072. Both measures are frequently reported together as in Table 7-2 below:

Table 7-2
Foreign Exchange Rates*

	Foreign Currency Units per U.S. $	U.S. $ Equivalents
Britain (pound)	.6144	1.6276
India (rupee)	16.5700	.0604
Japan (yen)	139.0800	.0072
South Korea (won)	670.8000	.0015
W. Germany (mark)	1.8917	.5286

*August 10, 1989

Currency Cross Rates

If we want to observe the exchange rate between two currencies, we could express everything in terms of cross rates:

Table 7-3
Currency Cross Rates*

	U.S. $	Mark	Won	Yen	Rupee	Pound
Britain	.6144	.3248	.0009	.0044	.0037	----
India	16.5700	8.7593	.0247	.1191	----	26.9694
Japan	138.0800	73.5212	.2073	----	8.3935	226.3672
S. Korea	670.8000	354.6017	----	4.8231	40.4829	1091.7100
W. Germany	1.8917	----	.0028	.0136	.1142	3.0789
U.S.	----	.5286	.0015	.0072	.0604	1.6276

*August 10, 1989

In the table above, the value of each currency unit is expressed in terms of other currencies. One U.S. dollar buys .6144 pounds, one mark buys .3248 pounds (.6144/1.8917 = .3248), and one pound buys 1.6276 U.S. dollars ($1/.6144 = 1.6276).

In Brief

Statistic	*Foreign Exchange*
Compiled by	Fed Board of Governors Leading financial newspapers
Frequency	daily
Release date	daily for newspapers, weekly for the Fed
Published data	*Fed Statistical Release H.10(510)* released Monday following previous week
Hotline update	None

Value of the Dollar

When we talk about the value of the dollar in the context of international trade or finance, we are usually referring to the number of other currency units that can be purchased with one U.S. dollar. The ratio between the two is called the *exchange rate.* There are well over 200 exchange rates in the world today.

The ***weighted average value of the U.S. Dollar*** is an index compiled by the Federal Reserve System which tracks the value of the U.S. dollar against a bundle of foreign currencies. It is the best overall measure of the strength of the dollar.

How Is the Weighted Average Computed?

To compile the index, the Fed selected a group of 10 major industrialized countries substantially involved in world trade.[2] The weight of each country's currency in the index is based on the amount of global trade each country had relative to the other countries in the sample right after flexible exchange rates were adopted in late 1971. After the relative weights were determined, the series was given a base of 100 for March 1973.

Since the series is in the form of an index, individual index values have no meaning other than in relation to the base or to other index numbers. When the index goes up, the dollar is getting stronger; when it goes down, the dollar is getting weaker relative to the currencies of the other 10 countries combined.

---

[2] Germany, Japan, France, United Kingdom, Canada, Italy, Netherlands, Belgium, Sweden, and Switzerland.

The Historical Record

The index is plotted in Figure 7-2 below. The data show that the index hit a low of 84.653 in July 1980 and a high of 158.430 in February 1985, a near doubling of the value of the dollar in a short period of time.

Figure 7-2
The Weighted Average Value of the U.S. Dollar

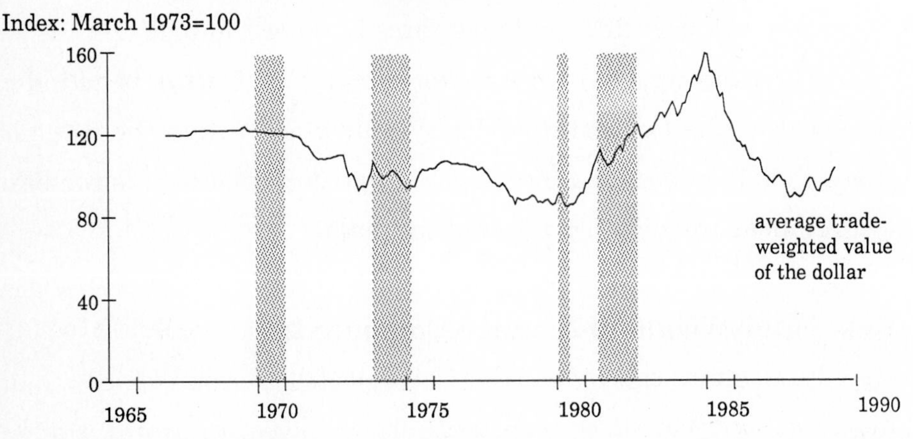

The value of the dollar is one of the main determinants of our import and export flows. When it is high, imports are inexpensive and our exports costly to foreign buyers. When the value of the dollar is low, the situation is exactly reversed. Imports become expensive, while our exports become less expensive for foreign buyers.

In Brief

Statistic	*Weighted Average Value of the U.S. Dollar*
Compiled by	The Fed Board of Governors
Frequency	Weekly
Release date	Week ended previous Friday
Published data	*Federal Reserve Bulletin* Foreign Exchange Rate releases H.10 (weekly), and G.5 (monthly)
Hotline update	None

Chapter 8
SOME FINAL WORDS ABOUT STATISTICS

Troubles With Numbers

The governments of the modern, industrialized nations of the free world -- the United States among the best of them -- enjoy a remarkable reputation for producing honest statistics. Surprisingly (since they bear less responsibility to the citizenry), so do many nongovernmental agencies in these countries that produce statistical series, some of which are included in this book. In some nations however, statistics are exaggerated, underreported, or simply faked for political or ideological reasons. When this happens, the usefulness of the statistics is radically reduced. Whether they know it or not, it is also a tragic loss to those nations that support this type of activity.

In the United States, it has sometimes been hinted that the release of new statistical figures was delayed for a few hours, in order to prevent some political or commercial embarrassment. But even such temporary mischief has not been widely confirmed. What no politician or business leader in America will deny is that statistics tend to be brutally honest.

The trouble with the numbers we are likely to use doesn't stem from outright fraud and dishonesty, but rather from ignorance or the "creative" use of numbers. And the single most common use of such creative policies is to tell only part of the statistical story, also known as "putting one's best foot forward."

This book warns against this practice repeatedly. For example, failing to account for inflation can give the impression that dollar amounts have grown, over the years, when they really haven't, or when they've grown very much less. Similarly, rising real GNP statistics look better before the attendant increased pollution and resource depletion (about which there are a few reliable statistics) are taken into account. In the same way, interest rates should always be put in the perspective of inflation and imports should be set against exports.

Indeed, telling the whole truth, giving the whole picture would be an unending task, because everything in the economy affects everything else. What we have to do is to draw the line somewhere and say, "These are the major considerations. Everything else has only insignificant relevance." But drawing lines is a contentious business, and that is one of the troubles we run into when using statistics.

Another problem is endowing statistics with significance they don't have. For example, a rising stock market, by itself, doesn't signal an economic expansion, nor do rising incomes or the increased international strength of the dollar. Some statistical series, interest rates very prominent among them, are often presented as leading indicators when they may more accurately be interpreted as lagging behind business conditions. And some statistics, such as foreign investment in American agriculture and industry, are trumpeted as indicators of impending disaster, when no such simple case can be made.

Perhaps at the root of these many troubles is that numbers often have a mystique about them. They are easily given more credibility than is their due. As mentioned in Chapter 1, their "scientific," "theoretical," or "official" nature tends to blind us to other realities. A healthy skepticism is good protection.

What to Look for in a Forecast

And then there are forecasts!

The motivating purpose behind much statistical analysis is to forecast the future. After all, once we know where we are, we usually want to know where we are going. As a result, we encounter many large and small forecasts in our daily lives, and these contain fertile opportunities for making statistical trouble.

The quintessential example of this might be the television weather forecaster that announces, say, a 30 percent chance of rain tomorrow, rising to an 80 percent change the day after tomorrow. At which point, the TV viewer should ask, does 30 percent mean it will rain seven hours and twelve minutes (30 percent) out of tomorrow's 24 hours everywhere in the station's viewing area, or does it mean that it will rain sometime tomorrow over 30 percent of the viewing area, or does it mean that it will rain somewhere, sometime tomorrow in the viewing area? And, by the way, is the forecast confined to the viewing area, and, if so, what is that area? Or is this a forecast generated for the distant city in which the weather service has its offices? And does tomorrow mean all 24 hours or only the waking hours? And would a slight drizzle count as rain? And ditto for all these questions for the day after tomorrow, when there is supposed to be an 80 chance of rain.

Apparently no one knows the answers to all these questions for sure, but weather forecasters continue to forecast this way. Perhaps they feel that it makes them seem more scientific, theoretical, and official.

So one thing to look for in forecasts is clarity and completeness of the forecasting statement. All questions like those above should be unnecessary. The forecast should not bite off more than it can chew (project too far in the future), it should be built on demonstrable logic, and it should have a sufficiently deep and broad statistical basis.

We are more likely to encounter other people's economic and business forecasts than to make these forecasts ourselves. Here are some things to look out for:

Point Forecasts These are the most common, but they are often wrong, because outcomes are unlikely to reach the predicted point precisely. For example, if we predict that GNP next year will be $6 trillion, we have an almost 100 percent chance of being wrong, because next year's GNP might turn up to $6 trillion and one cent or any other such number.

Interval Forecasts It is better to say that next year's GNP will be $6 trillion, give or take $50 billion. That means the forecast will turn out to be correct if next year's GNP falls between $5,950,000,000,000 and $6,050,000,000,000.

Probability Forecasts It is even better to say that next year's GNP has an 85 percent probability of being between

$5,950,000,000,000 and $6,050,000,000,000. This way the confidence with which the forecast is made can be expressed. The higher the probability, the more believable the forecast should be, assuming that the forecaster is reputable.

Unconditional Forecasts All of the above examples fall into this category, because, unlike the conditional forecast below, they are not premised on some second event taking place.

Conditional Forecasts "There is an 85 percent probability that next year's GNP will be between $5,950,000,000,000 and $6,050,000,000,000, if the Federal Reserve Banks don't raise their discount rates" is a conditional forecast. If the banks do, in fact, raise their discount rates, all bets are off.

Event Forecasts All the above examples fall into this category, because they deal with a single event, a single outcome.

Time Series Forecasts A series of forecasts that march into the future by some convenient time steps--weeks, months, quarters, or years--are much more complicated than a single-event forecast. For example, forecasting that, "the GNP next year will grow at an annual rate of 4 percent during the first six months and then slow to 3 percent in the last half of the year" is actually making at least two forecasts. Since the second one is probably dependent on the accurate outcome of the first, this kind of forecasting can be tricky. Rate-of-change-over-time forecasts are especially susceptible to this complication.

As with the aforementioned weather forecasts, too many of the forecasts we encounter in the daily news are not clear about what kind of forecast they are or how they have been constructed.

They often use hedging or waffling language that, when carefully read or listened to, pulls the rug of credibility out from underneath them.

Three Forecasting Techniques

Finally, it is reassuring to know that no matter how sophisticated they seem, forecasts can only be made in three ways.

One way is to continue an existing trend into the future. In its simplest version, we just extend current experience in a straight line. Obviously, this quick and dirty method is always eventually wrong. For example, if we continued to grow taller at the same rate we did when we were children, we would all be about twenty feet tall when we finally become old enough to retire.

Improving on this logic by building in forces that curve the straight-line extension, like adjusting for bullet drop and windage in gunsights, helps. But the complex forces that have to be built into economic and business forecasts are themselves too often unpredictable. The result is very sophisticated but very screwed up forecasts.

A second forecasting technique predicts the future as a returning cycle of the past. This was the basic premise of the first business cycle theories -- aptly named -- at the beginning of this century. It has a philosophic appeal, like the regular return of spring after winter and autumn after summer. But we know that "what goes up" does not necessarily ever have to "come down." Every day is new, every snowflake is different, and we cannot really turn either the clock or the calendar back.

Perhaps in exasperation, forecasts can also be based on hunch or educated guess. In fact, most forecasts contain some of this in their "smoothing" or even "fudge factors," especially when their other techniques would have produced forecasts that, while technically logical, would have been realistically off the deep end.

Good hunches and accurate educated guesses are, in fact, not illogical. They are mental processes that are so complex and sophisticated that they cannot be articulated as forecasting formulae. The trick is to be able to recognize when these hunches and guesses are good and accurate and when they are not.

All three forecasting techniques should be used, and a good forecast probably uses all of them simultaneously. Success is by no means guaranteed. Forecasting is an art as much as a science. Ironically, even the most poorly constructed forecasts can sometimes be surprisingly accurate, just like a clock that doesn't run but still tells the correct time twice a day.

Why We Need More than Statistics

We seem to be back where we started. Our own experience is our most immediate and direct indicator of how business and the economy are doing and how they are going to do.

There are two ways in which to make our experience more informative and more useful. The first is to become more aware of our economic and business environment, that is, to "raise our economic consciousness." Remember that we are alive and functioning in this environment, and our own eyes and ears are our best sources of information about it. Some things to look and listen for include increases or decreases in new residential and commercial building in our communities, in traffic patterns and congestion, and in shopping activity in local stores and malls. Perhaps it appears that there are more (or less) new cars on the road than usual. All of these observations can be made during the normal course of our daily activities, as can the changes in the levels of property maintenance -- whether or not houses need paint and lawns need tending -- of the homes in our communities. There are thousands of other kinds of observations we can make that may contribute to our accurate assessment of our economic and business situation.

The second way to make our own experience more information and useful is to learn more about how the economy functions, how its parts fit and work together, what impact government monetary and fiscal policies and government regulations have on business and the economy, how America participates in the global economy, and so forth. What is being recommended here, obviously, is the full-fledged study of economics. There really is no substitute. It can make sense out of the experiences we have that would otherwise yield only confusion.

Just as important, a solid grounding in economics can make the statistics come alive too. Admittedly, statistics -- the meat and potatoes of this book and the reason for its existence -- are almost universally regarded with a giant yawn. But tables of numbers and charts drawn on diagrams are only boring if they have no meaning. And as their meaning is revealed, they become very lively and very interesting indeed.

Index

Index